PLATEAU
MONT-ROYAL

W9-ARN-288

rue Roy

av. des Pins E.

av. Coloniale
rue De Bullion
av. de l'Hôtel-de-Ville
av. Laval
av. Henri-Julien
rue Drolet

av. De Châteaubri
rue Saint-Christophe
rue Bousquet

rue Cherrier

rue Prince-Arthur

rue Clark
boul. Saint-Laurent
rue Saint-Dominique

av. de l'Hôtel-de-Ville

Square
Saint-Louis

ITHQ

SHERBROOKE

rue Sherbrooke E.

rue Milton

rue Saint-Urbain

138

rue Sanguinet

rue Saint-Denis

rue Berri

rue Saint-Hubert
rue Saint-Christophe
rue Saint-André
rue Saint-Timothée
rue Amherst
rue Wolfe
rue De Montcalm
rue Beaudry

Saint-Norbert

Ontario

QUARTIER
LATIN

rue Robin

Grande
Bibliothèque

Station
Centrale

BEAUDRY

Place
des Arts

rue Clark

SAINT-
LAURENT

boul. De Maisonneuve E

UQAM

UQAM

BERRI-
UQAM

Place
Dupuis

VILLAGE

rue Sainte-Catherine E.

omplexe
esjardins

UQAM

UQAM

rue Saint-André

rue Amherst
rue Wolfe
rue De Montcalm
rue Beaudry

boul. René-Lévesque E.

omplexe
uy-Favreau

H
Hôpital
Saint-Luc

rue De La Gauchetière

rue Saint-Hubert

Maison de
Radio-Canada

CHINATOWN

boul. Saint-Laurent

av. Viger

Square Viger

autoroute Ville-Marie

PLACE-
D'ARMES

720

CHAMP-
DE-MARS

rue Saint-Antoine E.

rue Berri

rue Notre-Dame E.

rue Saint-Louis

Champ-de-Mars

rue du Champ-de-Mars

Banque
Montréal

ruelle des
Fortifications

Palais de
justice

Place
Armes

VIEUX-
MONTRÉAL

Former
Palais de
justice

Hôtel
de Ville

rue Notre-Dame E.

Sir-George-
Etienne-Cartier
National Historic Site

Basilique
otre-Dame

rue de
Brésoles

boul. St-Laurent

rue St-Jean-Baptiste

Édifice
Ernest-
Cormier

Ste-Thérèse

Château
Ramezay

Place
Jacques-
Cartier

rue Saint-Paul Est

rue Saint-Sulpice

rue St-Dizier

rue de la Commune

Marché
Bonsecours

Pointe-
à-Callière

OLD PORT

Bassin
Bonsecours

Bassin de l'Horloge

Quai
de l'Horloge

Tour de
l'Horloge

Quai des Convoyeurs

Quai
King-Edward

Bassin
Jacques-Cartier

Île Sainte-Hélène

Quai
Jacques-
Cartier

Longueuil

St. Lawrence River

Quai
Alexandra

Bassin
King-Edward

To arlene !

Fabulous Montréal

Experience the passion of **Montréal**!

Enjoy your stay

Ulysses Travel Guides

Publisher
Olivier Gougeon

Production Director
André Duchesne

Guide Update (taken from *Ulysses Travel Guide Montréal*) and Iconographic Research
Marie-Josée Guy

Update Contributor
Pierre Daveluy

Translator
Cindy Garayt

Computer Graphics
Pascal Biet
Marie-France Denis
Pierre Ledoux

Photography - Cover Page
Stéphan Poulin
A statue of a musician angel watches over the Notre-Dame-de-Bon-Secours chapel.

Acknowledgements

Ulysses Travel Guides would like to extend special thanks to Philippe B., Ligue nationale d'improvisation; Bernard Beauchemin, Mount Stephen Club; Linda Beaudin, World Trade Centre Montréal; Nathalie Belland, Nathalie Cooke, Tohu La Cité des arts du cirque; Suzanne Blais, Biosphère Environment Canada; Valérie Lafleur, Musée Marguerite-Bourgeoys; Nicole Bordeleau, Bentall Real Estate Services; Lise Buisson, RBC; Marie Caron, Place Ville Marie; Stéphane Chagnon, Maison nationale des Patriotes; Mélanie Crépeau, Quartierephemere.org; Mike Parente, Plaza Saint-Hubert; Jean-Louis Desrosiers, Collège Mont-Saint-Louis; Rhodnie Désir, Les Grands Ballets Canadiens de Montréal; Laurie Devine and Céline Poissant, McGill University; Sophie Dupont, Musée du Château Dufresne; Claire Ferland, Société du parc Jean-Drapeau; Marie-Joëlle Fillion, Montréal Botanical Garden and Insectarium; Pierre Gaufre, Société de développement de Montréal; André Gauvreau, Centre d'histoire de Montréal; Éric Gervais, Saute-Moutons; Sara Giguère, Musée du Château Ramezay; Éric Giroux, Écomusée du Fier Monde; Ginette Gratton, Société Radio-Canada; Cécile Grenier, Communauté Milton Parc; Mélissa Harvey, Montréal Biodôme and Planétarium; Hans J. Hofman, Redpath Museum; Nathalie Juteau, Old Port of Montréal Corporation; Gilbert Langlois, Musée des Hospitalières de l'Hôtel-Dieu de Montréal; Elizabeth Laurinaitis, Société de la Place des Arts; A. Légaré, Société du boulevard Saint-Laurent; Claude Lord, National Film Board of Canada Phototèque; Martin Maillet, Quartier international de Montréal; Erin Mark, Concordia University; Heather McNaab and Nike Langevin, McCord Museum of Canadian History; Audrey Messier Morissette, Just for Laughs; Andrew Mitchell, Canadian Centre for Architecture; Valérie Molenaar, Molson Canada; Coline Niess, Cinémathèque québécoise; Catherine Ordi, Bibliothèque nationale du Québec; Wanda Palma, Marie-Claude Saia and Linda-Anne D'Anjou, Montreal Museum of Fine Arts; Céline Perreault, Tourisme Montréal; Chantal Potvin, Cirque Éloize; Stéphan Poulin; Normand Prieur, Pascale Bergeron, Univers culturel de Saint-Sulpice; Francine Quesnel, Musée de Lachine; Marie-Claude Ravary, Québec Religious Heritage Foundation; Tudor Radulescu, Kanva Architecture; Philippe Renault; Christophe Riffaud, Danilo Baltodano, Élisabeth Pouliot-Roberge, Pointe-à-Callière musée d'archéologie et d'histoire de Montréal; Nancy Robert, Parquet-Centre CDP Capital; Johanne Robitaille, Julie Gazaille, Université de Montréal; Andrew Ross, City of Westmount; Monique Tairraz & Cie, communications; Françoise Théberge, Institut du Tourisme et d'Hôtellerie du Québec; Alain Tittley, Arrondissement d'Outremont; Réjean Tremblay, Orchestre Symphonique de Montréal; Nadine Viau, Ex-Centris.

We acknowledge the financial support of the Government of Canada through the Book Publishing Industry Development Program (BPIDP) for our publishing activities. We would also like to thank the Government of Québec – Tax credit for book publishing – Administered by SODEC.

Bibliothèque et Archives nationales du Québec and Library and Archives Canada cataloguing in publication

Main entry under title:

    Fabulous Montréal
    (Fabulous)
    Translation of: Fabuleux Montréal.
    Includes index.
    ISBN 978-2-89464-811-7
    1. Montréal (Québec) - Guidebooks. 2. Montréal (Québec) - Pictorial works. I. Series.

FC2947.18.F3213 2007   917.14'28045 C2006-941260-X

The city's downtown skyscrapers
sparkle with life as night falls.
© Grandmaisonc | Dreamstime.com

Table of Contents

Attraction Classification

★   Not to be missed
★ ★   Worth a visit
★ ★ ★   Interesting

The iridescent colours of the Palais des congrès de Montréal.
© Chantelle516 | Dreamstime.com

List of maps

The Promenade du Vieux-Port, a pleasant public space between the river and the city.

Where in the World?

Québec

Sept-Îles

Gaspé

CANADA

St. Lawrence River

Saguenay

Prince
Edward
Island

Charlottetown ⭐

New
Brunswick

Québec City

Fredericton ⭐

Ontario

Trois-Rivières

Halifax

Montréal

Nova
Scotia

Sherbrooke

Ottawa ✪

Toronto ⭐

Boston

Niagara
Falls

New York

UNITED STATES

Washington
D.C. ✪

Population

Metropolitan Area:
3,574,000 inhabitants

Island of Montréal:
1,814,170 inhabitants

Area

Island of Montréal: 499km²

Time Zone

GMT –5

Climate

Average temperature:
January: –10°C
(record low: –37.8°C
in 1957)

July: 21°C
(record high: 37.6°C
in 1975)

Average precipitation:
214cm of snow
736cm of rain

Highest Summit

Natural: Mount Royal,
at 233m

Urban: the 1000 De La
Gauchetière building, at 205m

Languages

Montréal is the second
largest Francophone city in
the world after Paris.

Percentage of population
for whom French is the first
language: 67,7%

Percentage of population
for whom English is the first
language: 12,6%

Allophone population: 19,7%

Cultural Diversity

More than a quarter of
Montréal's residents are
immigrants.

The city's largest ethnic
communities are Italian, Irish,
English, Scottish, Haitian,
Chinese and Greek.

PORTRAIT

Both Latin and Nordic, European and North American, cosmopolitan and metropolitan, the largest French-speaking city in the world after Paris and a bilingual hub, Montréal is definitely an exceptional city. Visitors to the city appreciate it for many different reasons; it succeeds in delighting American tourists with its European charm and also manages to surprise overseas travellers thanks to its haphazard character and nonchalance. Above all, Montréal holds nothing back and visitors often find what they are looking for without having to search too far.

Montréal is a city that seems to be caught between several different worlds: firmly planted in America yet looking towards Europe, claimed by two lands, Québec and Canada, and always, it seems, in the midst of social, economic and demographic changes.

It is difficult to define this city, especially since no postcard or cliché truly succeeds in evoking an image of it that is realistic or honest. If Paris has its great boulevards and squares, New York its skyscrapers and celebrated Statue of Liberty, what best symbolizes Montréal? Its numerous and beautiful churches, its Olympic Stadium, or its opulent Victorian residences?

Despite Montréal's rich architectural heritage, it is above all its unique, engaging atmosphere that appeals to people. Montréal is an enchanting city to visit and an exhilarating place to discover; it is generous, friendly and not at all mundane.

And when the time comes to celebrate jazz, film, comedy, francophone singers or Saint-Jean-Baptiste Day, hundreds of thousands of people flood into the streets, turning events into warm public gatherings. There is no doubt that Montréal is a big city that has managed to keep its human touch. For while its towering glass-and-concrete silhouette gives it the appearance of a North-American metropolis, Montréal has trouble hiding the fact that it is primarily a city of small streets and unique neighbourhoods, each with its own churches, businesses, restaurants, and bars—in short, its own personality, shaped over the years by the arrival of people from all corners of the globe.

Elusive and mysterious, Montréal is nevertheless genuine, and is as mystical for those who experience it on a daily basis as it is for visitors who are immersed in it for only a few days.

GEOGRAPHY

To fully understand Montréal's role in the history of the American continent, one must first look at the amazing assets of its location. Situated on an island in the St. Lawrence River, the main entry point to the American Northeast, Montréal stands on a spot where maritime traffic encounters its first major obstacle, the Lachine Rapids. Blocking all navigation, the rapids once forced navigators to stop in Montréal if they wished to travel any further on the river.

From an economic standpoint, this geographical quirk gave the site, both in Native times and during the French and British regimes, an undeniable advantage: that of being the first mandatory transhipment site on the river. Nature therefore irrevocably chose Montréal's vocation by making it the entrance to a vast territory and, consequently, a commercial crossroads for the whole continent.

Blue Montréal

The island of Montréal is formed by the St. Lawrence River and the Rivière des Prairies, which flows into the St. Lawrence at the eastern tip of the island. These two magnificent rivers are well known for the many islands that dot their waters.

Between Lac Saint-Louis, at the western tip of the island, and the Pointe-aux-Trembles neighbourhood to the east, the St. Lawrence River, which flows to the Atlantic Ocean, runs along the southern shore of the island. In the LaSalle borough, it suddenly becomes the tumultuous Lachine rapids.

Between Lac des Deux Montagnes, at the western tip of the island, and the Rivière-des-Prairies district, to the east, the Rivière des Prairies runs along the northern shore of the island. Its flow is controlled by the Rivière-des-Prairies hydroelectric power plant, in the Sault-au-Récollet sector.

Several bridges and the Louis-Hippolyte-La Fontaine tunnel link the island of Montréal to Île Jésus and the Montérégie and Lanaudière regions. Two métro tunnels also link the island to its two largest neighbouring cities, Laval to the north and Longueuil to the south.

The majestic St. Lawrence River provides Québec's metropolis with its distinctive insular character.
© Stéphan Poulin

THE MONTRÉAL ARCHIPELAGO

Some 11,500 years ago, the highest summits of the Montérégiennes hills, of which Mount Royal is part, emerged from the Champlain Sea. As the continent gradually came out of the water, the hills formed bigger and bigger islands. The island of Montréal came out 3,500 years later, right in the middle of what is called the "Montréal plain."

Today, the Montréal archipelago features over 300 islands, most of which are located at the confluence of the St. Lawrence and Ottawa rivers, such as Île Jésus (Laval), the second largest after the island of Montréal. The actual territory of Montréal is composed of some 80 islands, the main ones being, in decreasing order of size, the island of Montréal, Île Bizard, Nun's Island, and the Sainte-Hélène and Notre-Dame islands, both man-made for Expo 67.

Small islands were often immersed or submerged, or even used as pillars, such as the Îlot Normant. Now used as the foundation of the Alexandra pier, in the Old Port of Montréal, this islet was located right in front of the Place Royale. Swallowed by the waves, it probably did not hide any great treasures, but possibly an interesting page of history that has now disappeared. This small islet, named after Louis Normant de Faradon, superior of the Sulpicians in the 18th century, appears on various ancient maps depicting the port of Montréal by some 15 different appellations, such as Île du Marché (market island) and Île aux Huîtres (oyster island).

The port of Montréal, very busy in 1892 thanks to a deep channel that was dug in the St. Lawrence River to facilitate navigation to and from Québec City.
© M984.210 / McCord Museum, Montréal

Mount Royal is part of the Monteregian mountain chain that accentuates the St. Lawrence River plain in the background.
© Stéphan Poulin

Green Montréal

All around the island of Montréal, part of the St. Lawrence's and the Rivière des Prairies' shores have been, for the past few years, converted into green spaces. These public riverside parks, known as nature parks, are a great addition to the vast urban parks and multitude of small parks that are found in each of the island's neighbourhoods.

The most well-known and visible of Montréal's big parks is Mount Royal Park, whose spectacular size, right in the middle of the island, is definitely eye-catching. All year long, city dwellers climb to its summit for fun, to enjoy the view offered by its lookouts, or simply to keep fit.

A blend of untamed and domesticated nature, the Montréal Botanical Garden, one of the largest in the world, is located in the central eastern part of the island and welcomes both visitors and a wide array of bird species throughout the year. For its part, the Morgan Arboretum, a huge forest preserve located in the western part of the island, is home to various wild animals, including mammals, reptiles, amphibians and birds, in addition to majestic trees.

Portrait

Jacques Cartier encounters the Amerindian people of the village of Hochelaga for the first time in 1535. Champlain would find no trace of this community in 1603.

© M19656 / McCord Museum, Montréal

MONTRÉAL'S HISTORY

Origins

Before the regional balance was disrupted by the arrival of European explorers, what is known today as the island of Montréal was inhabited by the Iroquois nation. These people had probably recognized the location's exceptional qualities, which enabled it to flourish by dominating the St. Lawrence valley and by playing the role of commercial intermediary for the entire region.

In 1535 and 1541, Jacques Cartier, a navigator from Saint-Malo in the service of the king of France, became the first European to briefly explore the island. He took the opportunity to climb the mountain that rose out of its centre, which he christened *Mont Royal*. (Following Jacques Cartier's 1535 voyage, an Italian named Giovanni Battista Ramusio, born in 1485, analyzed Cartier's discoveries and published *Delle Navigationo et Viaggi* in 1556, a work that included a map of the Mount Royal region, called *La Terra de Hochelaga nella Nova Francia*, which he translated in Italian as *Monte Real*, the origins of "Montréal.")

In his ship's log, Cartier also mentioned a short visit to a large Aboriginal village apparently located on the side of the mountain. Inhabited by approximately 1,500 Iroquois, this village consisted of about 50 large dwellings protected by a high wooden palisade. All around, the villagers cultivated corn, squash and beans, thus meeting most of the dietary needs of their sedentary population. Unfortunately, Cartier left only a partial and sometimes contradictory account of this community, so that even today, the exact location of the village, as well as the name by which the Iroquois referred to it (Hochelaga or Tutonaguy), remain unknown.

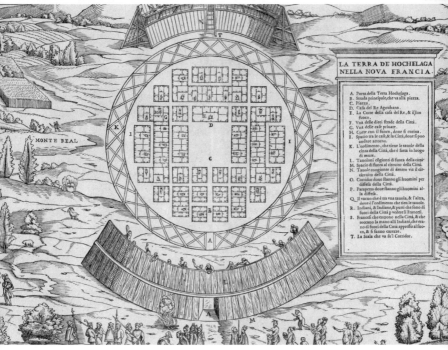

LA TERRA DE HOCHELAGA
NELLA NOVA FRANCIA.

A. Porta della Terra Hochelaga.
B. Strada principale, che va alla piazza.
C. Piazza.
D. Casa del Re Agouhana.
E. La Corte della casa del Re, & il suo fuoco.
F. Vna delle dieci strade della Città.
G. Vna delle case priuate.
H. Corte con il fuoco, doue si cucina.
I. Spacio tra le case, & la Città, doue si puo andare attorno.
K. L'ordinamento, che tiene le tauole della cinta della Città, che é fatta in luogo di mura.
L. Tauoloni congionti di fuora della città.
M. Spacio di fuora al circuito della Città.
N. Tauole congionte di dentro via il circuito della Città.
O. Corridor doue stanno gli huomini per diffeta della Città.
P. Parapetto doue stanno gli huomini alla diffefa.
Q. Il vacuo che é tra vna tauola, & l'altra, doue é l'ordimento che tien le tauole.
R. Indiani, & Indiane, & genti che sono di fuori della Città p vedere li Francesi.
S. Francesi che entrano nella Città, & che toccano la mano alli Indiani, che erano di fuori della Città appetto al fuoco, & si fanno carezze.
T. La Scala che va sù'l Corridor.

MONTE REAL

La terra de Hochelaga nella Nova Francia, drawn by Giovanni Battista Ramusio in 1565 after a description that was given by Jacques Cartier.
© Library and Archives Canada / NMC-1908

Another enduring mystery that still gives rise to much speculation is the astonishing and quick disappearance of this village after Cartier's visits. Some 70 years later, in 1603, when Samuel de Champlain travelled through the region, he found no trace of the Iroquoian community described by Cartier. The most popular hypothesis is that the Aboriginal people of the island of Montréal had fallen victim to trade rivals and finally been driven away from the island.

Champlain, the founder of New France, took an interest in the location's potential. In 1611, just three years after founding Québec City, he ordered that an area be cleared on the island. He viewed this spot, named Place Royale, as the starting point of a new colony or an outpost for the fur trade.

The project had to be postponed, however, since at the time the French, allied with the Algonquin and Huron, had to cope with attacks by the Five Nations of the Iroquois Confederacy. Supported by the merchants of New Amsterdam (which would later become New York), the Confederation was trying to seize complete control of the fur trade.

The founding of Montréal was thus delayed for a number of years and is not attributable to the efforts of Samuel de Champlain, who died in 1635.

Portrait

Ville-Marie (1642-1665)

The fur trade was the primary reason for the French colonization of Canada in those years; however, it does not appear to have been at the origin of the founding of Montréal.

The city, initially christened Ville-Marie, was established by a group of pious French men and women who were strongly influenced by the Jesuits' accounts of their time in America, as well as by the currents of religious revival that were then affecting Europe. Driven by idealism, they wanted to establish a small colony on the island in the hopes of converting natives and creating a new Christian society.

Jeanne Mance (1606-1673), founder of Montréal's Hôtel-Dieu hospital.
© *Library and Archives Canada / C-012329*

Paul de Chomedey, Sieur de Maisonneuve, was chosen to oversee this venture, and was later designated governor of the new colony. Heading an expedition of about 50 people, including Jeanne Mance, Maisonneuve arrived in America in 1641 and founded Ville-Marie in May of the following year. From the beginning, great efforts were made to hasten the construction of the social and religious institutions that would form the heart of the town. In 1645, work was begun on the Hôtel-Dieu, the hospital Jeanne Mance had dreamed about. A few years later, the first school was opened, under the direction of Marguerite Bourgeoys. The year 1657 was marked by the arrival of the first priests from the Séminaire de Saint-Sulpice in Paris, who subsequently, and for many years to come, had a decisive influence on the city's development. Ironically, the primary goal behind the founding of Ville-Marie, the conversion of the Iroquois, had to be abandoned, or at least set aside for a certain period of time. In fact, just one year after their arrival, the French had to confront the Iroquois, who feared that the presence of colonists would disrupt the fur trade and put them at a disadvantage.

Before long, a permanent state of war set in, threatening the very survival of the colony several times. Finally, however, after nearly a quarter-century of hanging by only a thread, the colony was provided with military protection by King Louis XIV, who had been governing New France himself for two years. From that point on, Ville-Marie, which had already come to be known as Montréal, began to flourish.

MAISONNEUVE, FOUNDER OF MONTRÉAL

In the 17th century, the fur trade was the driving force behind France's bid to colonize Canada. Yet this lucrative trade was not the initial cause of the founding of Montréal; rather, it was the religious conversion of First Nations peoples.

Paul de Chomedey, Sieur de Maisonneuve, born southeast of Paris in 1612, was not only chosen to carry out this mission, but also designated as the new colony's first governor. Maisonneuve left France in May 1641, leading an expedition of some 50 people, the Montréalistes de la Société Notre-Dame, a group that included Jeanne Mance. Jeanne Mance's ship reached Québec three months later without incident.

Maisonneuve was not so fortunate, however, encountering violent storms along the way. In fact, he arrived so late that the founding of Montréal was postponed to the following year, and the group spent winter in Québec City. On May 17, 1642, Maisonneuve founded Ville-Marie on the island of Montréal. A few years later, the name "Montréal" supplanted that of Ville-Marie.

In 1665, the governor of Montréal was summoned back to France indefinitely. He returned to Paris with a heavy heart, abandoning his duties and his beloved city and retiring among the Doctrine Chrétienne order of priests, where he died in 1676. He was likely buried in the order's former chapel, which was located in the vicinity of 17 Rue de Cardinal-Lemoine, in the 5e Arrondissement of Paris.

The founder of Montréal was a warm-hearted man of great intelligence and virtue. A monument to Paul de Chomedey, Sieur de Maisonneuve, erected in 1895, stands in Place d'Armes, in the heart of Old Montréal.

Maisonneuve, accompanied by the Montréalistes de la Société Notre-Dame, founds Ville-Marie on May 17, 1642.
© M976.179.3 / McCord Museum, Montréal

THE 1701 GREAT PEACE OF MONTRÉAL

When Lamothe de Cadillac founded the military post of Detroit in the summer of 1701, the Great Peace of Montréal treaty put an end to the conflict that raged between the French and their allies—the nations of the Upper Lakes region—and the Five Iroquois Nations. The negotiations brought together some 1,300 Native American delegates representing 40 Aboriginal nations, including the Iroquois, with whom everybody had been at war for a century. Peace reigned for 50 years.

Huron-Wendat chief Kondiaronk, who died on August 2, 1701 (two days before the ratification of the treaty), was one of the major participants in the peace negotiations. In his honour, the City of Montréal named the Chalet du Mont-Royal lookout after him in 1997.

The Fur Trade (1665-1760)

Although the church hierarchy still maintained its authority and the spiritual vocation of the town endured in people's minds, the protection afforded by the royal administration enabled Montréal to prosper as a military and commercial centre from 1665 on.

The arrival of French troops and the relative "pacification" of the Iroquois that ensued, especially after 1701 thanks to the signing of the Montréal peace treaty, finally made it possible to capitalize on the town's advantages as far as the fur trade was concerned. Since Montréal was the town located farthest up the St. Lawrence River, it soon surpassed Québec City as the hub of this lucrative commerce.

In addition, more and more young Montrealers called *coureurs des bois* were leaving the city and venturing deep into the hinterland to negotiate directly with native fur suppliers. Legalized in 1681, this practice gradually became more organized and hierarchical, and the *coureurs des bois* became for the most part paid employees of important Montréal merchants. Montréal, located at the gateway to the continent, also served as the starting point for France's intensive exploration of North America.

French expeditions, notably those led by Jolliet, Marquette, La Salle and La Vérendrye, kept pushing the borders of New France further and further. Pierre Le Moyne d'Iberville founded Louisiana in 1699, during one of these expeditions. In those years, France claimed the major part of present-day North America, an immense territory that enabled France to contain the expansion of the much more densely populated English colonies in the

south, between the At-
lantic and the Appala-
chians.

Supported by the
royal administration,
Montréal continued to
grow slowly through-
out this period. In
1672, a map was cre-
ated, delimiting for the
first time a number of
the city's streets, the
most important be-
ing Rue Notre-Dame
and Rue Saint-Paul.
Then, between 1717
and 1741, the wooden
palisade surrounding
the city was replaced
by a stone wall over
5m high to reinforce
the city's defences.

Montréal was a major hub in the lucrative fur trade during the
18th century.
© Library and Archives Canada / C-011013

While the population grew somewhat slowly, it nevertheless spread beyond
the areas outside the enclosure from the 1730s on. A clear social distinction
gradually developed between the residents of these areas and those of the
city centre, where, after a number of devastating fires, only stone buildings
were permitted. The core of the city, protected by walls, was occupied
mainly by members of the local aristocracy, wealthy merchants, and social
and religious institutions, while the outlying areas were inhabited primarily
by artisans and peasants. With its numerous multi-level stone houses, the
centre of Montréal already had the appearance and atmosphere of a small,
peaceful French city by the middle of the 18th century.

The Seven Years War, which raged through Europe between 1756 and
1763, had enormous repercussions in America, which quickly became
a battlefield. Québec City in 1759 and Montréal the following year fell
into the hands of British troops. When the war ended in Europe, France
officially ceded control of almost all its North-American possessions to
England under the Treaty of Paris, thereby signing New France's death
sentence. As a result, the fate of Montréal and its francophone population,
numbering 5,733 inhabitants, was significantly altered.

Transitional Years (1763-1850)

The first decades after the conquest (1759-1760) were characterized by
an atmosphere of uncertainty for the city's community. First of all, despite the return of a civilian government in 1764, French-speaking citizens
continued to be edged out and excluded from public administration and
higher realms of decision-making, until 1774, when control of the lucra-

Portrait

THE WOMEN
OF NEW FRANCE

Marguerite Bourgeoys.   © M930.50.8.136 / McCord Museum, Montréal

Montréal would not be what it is today if there had not been among its founders and benefactors courageous women inspired by faith and devotion. A minority in a man's world, these women still succeeded in imposing their ideas and their vision. In addition, they played a major role and actively participated in the community's development. And let's not forget the *Filles du Roy* (the king's daughters), women who were determined to make a new life for themselves and who are the ancestors of a majority of Montrealers.

Jeanne Mance arrived in Montréal on May 17, 1642. The right arm of Sieur de Maisonneuve, she is associated with the founders of Ville-Marie in the Société de Notre-Dame de Montréal. Mandated by her protector, benefactor Madame de Bullion, she established the Hôtel-Dieu de Montréal hospital in October of 1642 and, in 1659, brought the Hospitalières de Saint-Joseph from France.

Having left France with the *Grande Recrue* ("Great Recruitment"), Marguerite Bourgeoys settled in Montréal in 1653. She had a wood chapel built on the site that is now the Notre-Dame-de-Bon-Secours chapel. In 1658, she opened the first school for girls in Ville-Marie, and in 1671, she obtained a letter from the king allowing her to establish the Congregation of Notre-Dame.

Widowed at a young age, Madame d'Youville (Marie-Marguerite Dufrost de Lajemmerais) founded the Sisters of Charity of Montréal on December 31, 1737. Also known as the Grey Nuns, they were the first religious community to be founded by a Canadian woman. Mother d'Youville made a commitment, along with three female associates, to dedicate herself to the poor.

An important centre of commerce in 1830, Montréal's port attracted both European sailboats and Native canoes.
© M303 / McCord Museum, Montréal

tive fur trade passed into the hands of the conquerors, particularly a small group of merchants of Scottish extraction who would go on to form the Northwest Company in 1787.

In 1775-1776, the city was invaded once again, this time by American troops, who only stayed a few months. It was therefore at the end of the American Revolution that Montréal and other parts of Canada were faced with the first large waves of English-speaking immigrants, the Loyalists (American colonists wishing to maintain their allegiance to the British Crown). Later, from 1815 on, these individuals were followed by large numbers of newcomers from the British Isles, especially Ireland, which at the time was severely stricken by famine. The French-Canadian population, meanwhile, was growing at a remarkable pace due to a very high birth rate.

This rapid increase in the Canadian population had a positive effect on Montréal's economy as the urban and rural areas grew more and more dependent upon one another. The rapidly expanding rural areas, particularly in the part of the territory that would later become Ontario, formed a lucrative market for all sorts of products manufactured in Montréal. The country's agricultural production, particularly wheat, which inevitably passed through the port of Montréal before being shipped to Great Britain, ensured the growth of the city's port activities. Then, in 1825, an old dream was realized with the inauguration of a canal that made it possible to bypass the Lachine rapids.

Portrait

The capital of United Canada since 1844, Montréal lost its status following the burning of its parliament building in 1849.

In fact, Montréal's economy was already so diversified by that time that it was barely affected when, in 1821, the Hudson's Bay Company took over the Northwest Company, which had represented the city's interests in the fur trade until then. For many years the mainspring of Montréal's economy, the fur trade had become but one industry among many.

In the 1830s, Montréal earned the title of most populated city in the country, surpassing Québec City. A massive influx of English-speaking colonists disrupted the balance between French and English, and for 35 years, starting in 1831, there was an anglophone majority in Montréal.

Furthermore, the city's different ethnic communities had already started to band together in a pattern that would endure for many years to come: francophones lived mainly in the east end, while the Irish stayed in the southwest and the Anglo-Scottish remained in the west. These various ethnic groups did not, however, share the territory without problems. When the *Patriote* rebellions broke out in 1837-1838, Montréal became the scene of violent confrontations between the members of the Doric Club, composed of loyal British subjects, and the *Fils de la Liberté* (Sons of Liberty), made up of young francophones. It was actually after an inter-ethnic riot, leading to a fire that destroyed the parliament building, that Montréal lost its six-year-old title of capital of United Canada in 1849.

Although Montréal's urban landscape did not undergo any major changes during the first years of the English Regime, British-style buildings gradually began to appear in the 1840s. It was also at this time that the city's wealthiest merchants, mainly of Anglo-Scottish descent, gradually abandoned the Saint-Antoine neighbourhood and settled at the foot of Mount Royal. From that point on, less than a century after the conquest (1759-1760), the British presence became an undeniable part of the city's makeup. It was also at this time that a crucial phase of Montréal's development began.

Portrait

Industrialization and Economic Power (1850-1914)

Montréal experienced the most important period of growth in its history from the second half of the 19th century until World War I, thanks to rapid industrialization that began in the 1840s and continued in waves. From then on, the city ranked as Canada's undisputed metropolis and became the country's true centre of development.

An advertisement for Montréal's oldest foundry, the Eagle Foundry, established in 1823.

© M930.50.3.134 / McCord Museum, Montréal

The broadening of Canada's internal market—first with the creation of United Canada in 1840 and then, more importantly, the advent of Canadian Confederation in 1867—reinforced Montréal's industrial sector, whose products were increasingly replacing imports. The main forces that would long lie at the heart of the city's economy were the shoe, clothing, textile and food industries, as well as certain heavy industries, particularly rolling stock and iron and steel products. The geographical concentration of these activities near the port facilities and railroad tracks significantly altered the city's appearance.

The area around the Lachine Canal, the cradle of Canada's industrial revolution, followed by the Sainte-Marie and Hochelaga neighbourhoods, filled up with factories and inexpensive housing intended for workers. The industrialization of Montréal was intensified by the city's advantageous position as a transportation and communications hub for the entire Canadian territory, a position it worked to strengthen throughout this period. For example, starting in the 1850s, a channel was dug in the river between Montréal and Québec City, enabling larger ships to go up-river to the metropolis and eliminating most of the advantages enjoyed by Québec City's port.

The railroad network that was beginning to extend over the Canadian territory also benefited Montréal by making the city the centre of its activities. Montréal's industries enjoyed privileged access to the markets of southern Québec and Ontario via the Grand Trunk network, and the west of the country via that of Canadian Pacific, which reached Vancouver in 1887. As far as both domestic and international trade were concerned, Montréal occupied a dominant position in the country during this period.

THE LACHINE CANAL: THEN AND NOW

The mainspring of Montréal's industrialization, the 14.5km-long Lachine Canal has been part of the city's heritage since the 19th and 20th centuries, when its excavation and the building of its sluice gates made it possible to bypass the tumultuous Lachine Rapids, after a few fruitless attempts.

François Dollier de Casson, the Superior of the Sulpician order, was the first, in 1689, to believe in the project of a canal bypassing the rapids and leading to the Great Lakes. The project was ultimately abandoned in midstream due to high costs. After the conquest of New France, a similar project was undertaken by the British and, after seven years of studies, negotiations and petitions, was completed between 1812 and 1819.

It was then that Montréal merchants formed the Company of the Lachine Canal in order to finally complete the present canal. The company went bankrupt in 1821, but the project was taken over and the work completed by the government of Lower Canada. The widening of the canal, as well as the restoration and addition of locks, would proceed without interruption between its opening in 1825 and that of the St. Lawrence Seaway in 1959. The Lachine Canal was closed to maritime traffic between 1970 and 2002, when it re-opened to pleasure boats for summer.

A cradle of Canadian industry, the Lachine Canal was dug between the port of Montréal and Lachine's Lac Saint-Louis.
© M984.273 / McCord Museum, Montréal

The city's rapid growth was equally exceptional from a demographic point of view; between 1852 and 1911, the population went from 58,000 to 468,000 (528,000 including the suburbs). This remarkable increase was due to the huge pull of the booming city. The massive waves of immigration from the British Isles, which had begun in the early 19th century, continued for several more years before slowing down significantly during the 1860s. This deceleration was then amply compensated for by an exodus of peasants from the Québec countryside, attracted to Montréal by the work offered in its factories.

Grand Trunk established a railway link with the Atlantic Coast by building Montréal's Victoria Bridge in 1860.
© M969.81 / McCord Museum, Montréal

The arrival of this mainly francophone population also led to a new reversal of the balance between French and English in Montréal. By 1866, the population became, and remains to this day, mainly francophone. An entirely new phenomenon began to take shape toward the end of the 19th century, when Montréal started

At the start of the 20th century, the residents of the fast-developing city of Montréal find their cityscape steadily invaded by a tangle of electrical wires.
© MP-0000.813.1 / McCord Museum, Montréal

attracting immigrants from places other than France and the British Isles. Initially, those who came in the greatest numbers were Eastern European Jews fleeing persecution in their own countries. At first, they grouped together mainly along Boulevard Saint-Laurent.

A considerable number of Italians also settled in Montréal, mostly, for their part, in the northern section of the city. Thanks to these waves of immigration, Montréal already had a decidedly multi-ethnic character by 1911, with more than 10% of its population neither of British nor French extraction.

The urbanization resulting from this population growth caused the city to spread out further, a phenomenon promoted by the creation of a streetcar network in 1892. The city thus expanded beyond its old limits on a number of occasions, annexing up to 31 new territories between 1883 and 1918.

At the same time, efforts were being made to lay out areas where Montrealers could spend leisure time, such as Mount Royal Park (1874). As far as residential construction was concerned, British-inspired styles were most prevalent, notably in working-class neighbourhoods, where row houses with flat roofs and brick fronts predominated.

Portrait

Furthermore, in order to offer low-cost housing to working-class families, these buildings frequently had two or three stories and were designed to accommodate at least as many families. Affluent Montrealers were increasingly settling on the flanks of Mount Royal, in a neighbourhood that would soon be known as the Golden Square Mile due to the great wealth of its residents.

The Mount Royal Observatory neighboured the lookout in 1906. It was replaced by the mountain's current chalet in 1931.
© MP-0000.1750.8.2 / McCord Museum, Montréal

The industrial revolution had increased the socio-economic divisions within Montréal society. This phenomenon separated the main ethnic groups involved in an almost dichotomous fashion, since the upper middle class was almost entirely made up of Anglo-Protestants, while the majority of unspecialized workers consisted of French and Irish Catholics.

Between the Two Wars

From 1914 to 1945, a number of international-scale events hindered the city's growth and evolution. First of all, with the beginnings of World War I in 1914, Montréal's economy stagnated due to a drop in investments. It regained strength very quickly, however, thanks to the exportation of agricultural products and military equipment to Great Britain.

But those years were mostly marked in Montréal by a political battle waged between anglophones and francophones on the subject of the war. Francophones had mixed feelings about the British Empire and therefore protested at length against any Canadian participation in the British war effort. They were fiercely opposed to the conscription of Canadian citizens.

Anglophones, many of whom still had very strong ties with Great Britain, were in favour of Canada's full involvement. When, in 1917, the Canadian government finally made a decision and imposed conscription, francophones exploded with anger and Montréal was shaken by intense inter-ethnic tensions.

The war was followed by a few years of economic readjustment, and then by "the Roaring Twenties," a period of sustained growth stretching from 1921 to 1929. During this time, development in Montréal picked up where it had left off before the war, and the city maintained its role as Canada's

A peaceful anti-conscription demonstration crosses downtown Montréal on its way to Square Victoria on May 24, 1917.

© Library and Archives Canada / C-006859

metropolis. Toronto, however, thanks to American investments and the development of Western Canada, was already starting to claim a more important place for itself.

Taller and taller buildings with designs reflecting American architectural trends gradually began to appear in Montréal's business centre. The city's population also started growing again, so much so that by the end of the 1920s, there were over 800,000 people living in Montréal, while the population on the island as a whole had already exceeded the one-million mark. Due to both the size of its population and the appearance of its business centre, Montréal already had all the attributes of a major North-American city.

The crisis that struck the world economy in 1929 had a devastating effect on Montréal, whose wealth was mainly based on exports. For an entire decade, poverty was widespread in the city, as up to a third of the population of working age was unemployed.

This dark period did not end until the beginning of World War II, in 1939. From the start of this conflict, however, the controversy surrounding the war effort was rekindled, once again dividing the city's francophone and anglophone populations. The mayor of Montréal, Camillien Houde, who was opposed to conscription, was actually imprisoned between 1940 and 1944. Ultimately, Canada became fully involved in the war, putting its industrial production and army of conscripts at Great Britain's disposition.

Portrait

Renewed Growth (1945-1960)

After many years of rationing and unfavourable upheavals, Montréal's economy emerged from the war stronger and more diversified than ever. What followed was a prosperous period during which the population's consumer demands could be met. For more than a decade, unemployment was almost nonexistent in Montréal, and the overall standard of living improved radically.

The growth of the Montréal urban area was equally remarkable from a demographic point of view, so much so that between 1941 and 1961, the population practically doubled, going from 1,140,000 to 2,110,000, while the population of the city itself passed the one-million mark in 1951. This population explosion had several causes, first of which was the century-old exodus of rural inhabitants to the city, more widespread than ever, which resumed after coming to an almost complete halt during the Great Depression and World War II. Immigration also recommenced, the largest groups now arriving from southern Europe, especially Italy and Greece.

In the heart of the metropolis: Rue Sherbrooke in the mid-1950s.
© MP-1984.6.1.1 / McCord Museum, Montréal

The increase in Montréal's population was also due to a sharp rise in the number of births, a veritable baby boom that affected Québec as much as it did the rest of North America. To meet the housing needs of this population, neighbourhoods located slightly on the outskirts of the city were quickly covered with thousands of new homes. In addition, suburbs even further removed from the downtown area emerged, fostered by the popularity of the automobile as an object of mass consumption. Suburbs also began developing off the island on the south shore of the river, around the access bridges, and to the north, on Île Jésus, now known as Laval. At the same time, downtown Montréal underwent some important changes, as the business section gradually shifted from Old Montréal to the area around Boulevard René-Lévesque (formerly Boulevard Dorchester), where ever more imposing skyscrapers were springing up.

During this same period, the city was affected by a wave of social reforms aiming, in particular, at putting an end to the "reign of the underground." For years, Montréal had had a well-deserved reputation as a place where prostitution and gambling clubs flourished, thanks to the blind eye of some corrupt police officers and politicians. A public inquiry conducted between 1950 and 1954, during which lawyers Pacifique Plante and Jean Drapeau stood out in particular, led to a series of convictions and a significant improvement in the social climate.

THE *REFUS GLOBAL*

"Supporters of the status quo suspect us of endorsing the 'Revolution,' supporters of the 'Revolution' of being mere rebels: '... we oppose the established order, but only to transform it, not change it.'"

Extract from the *Refus Global* manifesto, 1948
Paul-Émile Borduas and 15 other signatories

The *Refus Global*, which spawned the Quiet Revolution of the 1960s, is a manifesto denouncing the political and religious conformity of the 1940s, which made Québec a stifling and hostile environment hindering individual and collective creativity. Signed in 1948 by painter Paul-Émile Borduas (1905-1960) and 15 other artists including Jean-Paul Riopelle, the manifesto marked the beginning of a radical shift in Québec society. Following its publication, which caused a huge uproar, Borduas was fired from his teaching post at Montréal's École du Meuble and, a few years later, sought exile in Paris.

At the same time, a desire for change manifested itself in strong protests by Montréal's francophone intellectuals, journalists and artists against the all-powerful Catholic Church and the pervading conservatism of the times. However, the most striking phenomenon of this period remained French-speaking Montrealers' nascent awareness of their alienation. Indeed, over the years, save certain exceptions, a very clear socio-economic split had developed between the city's two main groups.

Francophones earned lower average incomes than their anglophone colleagues, were more likely to hold subordinate positions, and their attempts at climbing the social ladder were mocked. And though the francophone population formed a large majority, Montréal projected the image of an Anglo-Saxon city due to its commercial signs and the supremacy of the English language in the main spheres of economic activity. It wasn't until the early 1960s that the desire for change evolved into a series of accelerated transformations.

Portrait

From 1960 to Today

The 1960s were marked by an unprecedented reform movement in Québec, a veritable race for modernization and change in various fields that soon became known as the Quiet Revolution. The baby boom of the previous decades considerably increased the population of Québec, both in the metropolis and in the regions. The suburbs of several cities became home to a high number of young couples, but for Montréal in particular, it became imperative to redevelop the urban space to maintain a prosperous economy. However, in the mid-1970s, Montréal lost its title of Canadian metropolis to Toronto, which, for a while now, had enjoyed more considerable growth. The appearance of more and more skyscrapers in the downtown core nonetheless showed that Montréal's economy continued to grow strong.

Aside from the suburban exodus, another phenomenon was taking place: the "back-to-the-land" movement. This trend, which lasted until the early 1980s, brought young people from all walks of life, mainly from the city, together in "communes." These communities usually numbered several families who shared farm chores in a spirit of openness and sharing.

At the same time, Montréal, whose mayor at the time was Jean Drapeau, shone brightly on the international scene as the city inaugurated its metro system and played host to a number of large-scale events, the most noteworthy being the 1967 World's Fair (Expo 67), the 1976 Summer Olympic Games and the 1980 Floralies Internationales (International Flower Show).

The Biosphère, formerly Expo 67's United States pavilion.
© Yanive Nizard Lafrance | Dreamstime.com

In this climate of economic change, the linguistic and cultural presence of French developed, and throughout the years, the voice of the French-speaking population became louder in Montréal. Unions and students staged protests to voice their discontent, while General Charles de Gaulle's famous declaration of *"Vive le Québec libre!"* (Long live a free Québec!) from the balcony of City Hall solidified the now well-defined idea of a sovereign Québec.

Starting in 1963, the Front de Libération du Québec (FLQ) had organized a series of terrorist attacks in the metropolis. The most dramatic event was the October Crisis of 1970, when British diplomat James Cross was kidnapped and released two months later, and Pierre Laporte, a minister in the Québec government, was killed. Nearly 40 years later, this sombre chapter of Québec history remains the subject of heated debates.

Montréal's Universal Exposition: Expo 67.
© Le Québec en images

The city's image changed noticeably, as commercial signage, until then strictly in English or occasionally in both languages, became exclusively French thanks to linguistic laws that were passed by successive provincial governments. For many English speakers, these laws, combined with the rise of nationalism and Québécois entrepreneurship, were changes that were too difficult to accept; many left Montréal and the province for good to settle in other Canadian cities or in the United States.

During the 1980s and 1990s, Montréal's economy underwent profound changes with the decline of many branches of activity that had shaped its industrial structure for over a century. These were then partially replaced by massive investments in such leading industries as aeronautics, computers and pharmaceutical products. However, this new economic growth was mostly beneficial to the city's ever-spreading suburbs.

In other developments, the previous decades' influx of immigrants from around the world transformed Montréal into an increasingly complex cultural mosaic. More than ever, it had become a true international crossroads, while retaining the enviable title of North-American metropolis of French culture.

MONTRÉAL'S COMMUNITIES

Saturday night, on Rue Durocher in Outremont, dozens of Hasidic (orthodox) Jews dressed in traditional garb hurry to the nearby synagogue. A few hours earlier, as usual, a portion of Montréal's large Italian community met at Marché Jean-Talon to negotiate the purchase of products imported directly from Italy or simply to socialize with compatriots and discuss the latest soccer game between Milan and Turin.

Portrait

MULTICULTURAL MONTRÉAL

Nearly half of Montréal's immigrants, who represent about 30% of the city's population, are of Italian origin, but this ethnic group is only one of 125 cultural communities found in the city. Most Montrealers recognize the contributions of these communities to the province's economic, social and cultural growth, and have developed affinities in diverse fields with their fellow citizens from other parts of the world.

These new Québécois, the majority of whom have successfully integrated Montréal society, only wish to find their place in the sun. Many must learn French and some are forced to go back to school, all the while confronting various prejudices. Montrealers nonetheless generally appreciate these newcomers and love to take part in their festivals and savour their delicious cuisines.

These scenes, well known to all Montrealers, are only two examples of the vital community life of a number of the city's ethnic groups. In fact, Montréal's ethnic communities have countless meeting places and associations. One need only take a brief stroll down Boulevard Saint-Laurent, also known as The Main, which divides the city between east and west and is lined with restaurants, grocery stores and other businesses with an international flavour, to be convinced of the richness and diversity of Montréal's population.

Indeed, Montréal often seems like a heterogeneous group of villages, which, without being ghettos, are mainly inhabited by members of one ethnic community or another. This sectioning of the city was initiated back in the 19th century by Montrealers of French and English descent—a division that still marks the city to a certain degree.

The east thus remains to a large extent francophone, while the west is anglophone. The most affluent members of the two communities live for the most part on opposite sides of Mount Royal, in Outremont and Westmount. With the arrival of immigrants from different ethnic backgrounds, several new neighbourhoods gradually fit into this puzzle. Very early, a small Chinese community, whose members had come to work in Canada when the railroads were being built, took up residence around Rue de la Gauchetière, west of Boulevard Saint-Laurent, which remains Montréal's Chinatown to this day.

The city's large Jewish community, for its part, first gathered a little higher on Boulevard Saint-Laurent and then settled further west, particularly in certain parts of Outremont, Côte-des-Neiges and Snowdon and in the municipalities of Côte-Saint-Luc and Hampstead, where its institutions flourished. Little Italy, often a very lively and colourful place with many cafés, restaurants and shops, occupies a large section in the northern part of the city, near Rue Jean-Talon and the Saint-Léonard area, where many Italians live. Italians actually make up Montréal's largest ethnic community and add an undeniable energy to the city.

Finally, a number of other more recently established communities also tend to gather in certain areas; for example, Greeks along

Chinatown's huge multicoloured gates provide a taste of Imperial China in downtown Montréal.
© iStockphoto.com

Avenue du Parc, Haitians in the Saint-Michel neighbourhood, Portuguese around Rue Saint-Urbain and Jamaicans in Griffintown. In Montréal, it seems as if you almost travel from one country to another within the space of a few blocks.

Furthermore, today's Italian Montrealers no longer live in Little Italy, just as the Chinese no longer live in Chinatown. Most of Montréal's districts are characterized by the presence of several ethnic communities living in harmony. However, tension and friction, caused by misunderstandings and prejudice, have not completely disappeared. Adjustments are still necessary, especially in schools, but in general, Montréal has a true atmosphere of understanding. This cultural mosaic represents one of the city's greatest riches.

The Jacques Cartier Bridge, inaugurated in 1930.

EXPLORING

Rue University, one of the Quartier International de Montréal's main arteries. © Stéphan Poulin

Vieux-Montréal

The unique historical and cultural setting of Vieux-Montréal's narrow streets provides the ideal point of departure for visitors to launch their exploration of the city.

In the 18th century, Montréal, like Québec City, was surrounded by stone fortifications. Between 1801 and 1817, these ramparts were demolished by local merchants who saw them as an obstacle to the city's development. The network of old streets, compressed after nearly a century of confinement, nevertheless remained in place. Today's Vieux-Montréal, or Old Montréal, thus corresponds quite closely to the area covered by the fortified city.

© Stéphan Poulin

The narrow cobblestone streets of Old Montréal are the perfect setting for a romantic stroll.

© iStockphoto.com

The elegant Tour de l'Horloge was erected in 1922 to honour the merchant marine sailors who died during World War I.

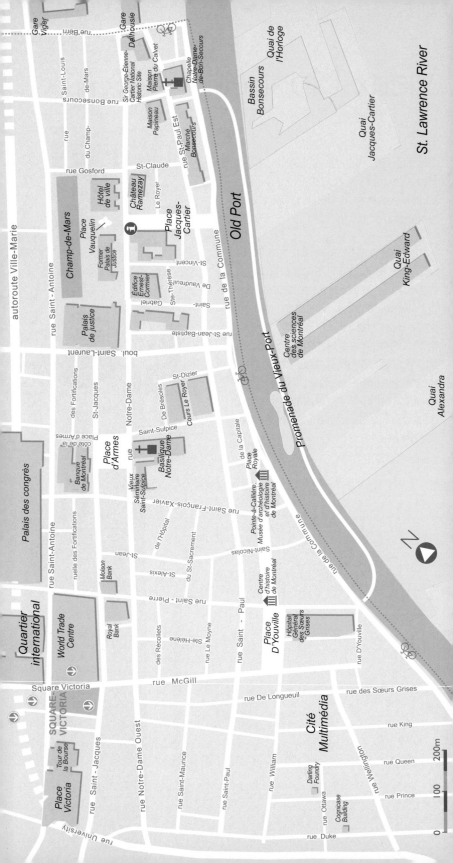

A walk through the cobblestone streets of Old Montréal provides a glimpse into the city's storied past.
© iStockphoto.com / Victor Kapas

During the 19th century, the city became the hub of commercial and financial activity in Canada. Banks and insurance companies built sumptuous head offices here, leading to the demolition of almost all buildings erected under the French Regime.

The area was later abandoned for nearly 40 years in favour of today's modern downtown area. Finally, the long process of breathing new life into Old Montréal got underway during the preparations for Expo 67 and continues today with numerous conversion and restoration projects. This revitalization has even gotten a second wind since the late 1990s. In fact, several high-end hotels have been established in historic buildings, while many Montrealers have rejuvenated the neighbourhood by making it their home.

The modern-day downtown area, where glass and steel skyscrapers tower over wide boulevards, marks a sharp contrast with the old part of the city where stone buildings predominate on narrow, compact streets.

Rue Saint-Jacques was the main artery of Canadian high finance for over a century. This role is reflected in its rich and varied architecture, which serves as a veritable encyclopedia of styles from 1830 to 1930. In those years, the banks, insurance companies and department stores, as well as the nation's railway and shipping companies, were largely controlled by Montrealers of Scottish extraction, who had come to the colonies to make their fortune.

Begun in 1928 according to plans by New York skyscraper specialists, the former head office of the **Banque Royale / Royal Bank** ★★ was one of the last buildings to be erected during this era of prosperity. The 23-storey tower has a base inspired by Florentine palazzos, which corresponds to the scale of neighbouring buildings. Inside the tower, visitors can admire the high ceilings of this "temple of finance," built at a time when banks needed impressive

Vieux-Montréal

buildings to win customers' confidence. The walls of the great hall are emblazoned with the heraldic insignia of eight of the 10 Canadian provinces, as well as those of Montréal (St. George's Cross) and Halifax (a yellow bird), where the bank was founded in 1861.

The **Banque Molson / Molson Bank** ★ was founded in 1854 by the Molson family, famous for the brewery established by their ancestor, John Molson (1763-1836), in 1786. Completed in 1866, the bank's head office was one of the earliest canadian examples of the Second Empire, or Napoleon III, style. This French style, modelled on the Louvre and the Paris Opera, was extremely popular in North America between 1865 and 1890. Above the entrance, visitors will see the sandstone carvings of the heads of William Molson and two of his children. The Molson Bank, like other banks at the time, even printed its own paper money—an indication of the power wielded by its owners, who contributed greatly to the city's development.

Under the French Regime, **Place d'Armes** ★★ was the heart of the city. Used for military manoeuvres and religious processions, the square was also the location of the Gadoys well, the city's main source of potable water. In 1847, the square was transformed into a lovely, fenced-in Victorian garden, which was destroyed at the beginning of the 20th century to make room for a tramway terminal. In the meantime, a **monument to Maisonneuve** ★★ was erected in 1895. Executed by sculptor Philippe Hébert, it shows the founder of Montréal, Paul de Chomedey, Sieur de Maisonneuve, surrounded by prominent figures from the city's early history, namely Jeanne Mance, founder of the Hôtel-Dieu hospital, Lambert Closse and his dog Pilote, and Charles Le Moyne, the head of a family of famous explorers. An Iroquois warrior completes the tableau.

The Royal Bank building as seen from Rue Saint-Jacques in 1930.
© RBC

The stunning lobby of the Royal Bank's former head office.
© RBC

A monument honouring city founder Paul de Chomedey, Sieur de Maisonneuve, stands in the heart of Place d'Armes.
© Denis Tremblay

The square is surrounded by several noteworthy buildings. The **Banque de Montréal ★ ★**, or Bank of Montreal, founded in 1817 by a group of merchants, is the country's oldest banking institution. Its present head office takes up an entire block on the north side of Place d'Armes. A magnificent building created by John Wells in 1847 and modelled after the Roman Pantheon, it occupies the place of honour in the centre of the block. Its Corinthian portico is a monument to the commercial power of the Scottish merchants who founded the institution. The columns' capitals, for their part, were severely damaged by pollution and replaced in 1970 with aluminum replicas. The pediment includes a bas-relief depicting the bank's coat of arms carved out of Binney stone in Scotland by Her

Majesty's sculptor, Sir John Steele. The interior was almost entirely redone in 1904-05. On this occasion, the bank was endowed with a splendid banking hall, designed in the style of a Roman basilica, with green syenite columns, gilded bronze ornamentation and beige marble counters.

The former **New York Life Building**, a surprising red-sandstone tower that was erected in 1888 for the insurance company, is regarded as Montréal's first skyscraper, even though it only has eight floors. The stone used for the facing was imported from Scotland. The building next door is adorned with beautiful Art Deco details. It was one of the first buildings over 10 stories to be erected in

Vieux-Montréal

Come nightfall, Place d'Armes dons its coat of lights. © Stéphan Poulin

Vieux-Montréal

Montréal after a regulation restricting the height of structures was repealed in 1927.

In 1663, the seigneury of the island of Montréal was acquired by the Sulpicians from Paris, who remained its undisputed masters up until the British conquest of 1759-1760. In addition to distributing land to colonists and laying out the city's first streets, the Sulpicians were responsible for the construction of a large number of buildings, including Montréal's first parish church (1673). Dedicated to *Notre Dame* (Our Lady), this Baroque church faced straight down the centre of the street of the same name, creating a perspective characteristic of classical French town planning. At the beginning of the 19th century, however, this rustic little church cut a sorry figure when compared to the Anglican cathedral on Rue

Notre-Dame and the new Catholic cathedral on Rue Saint-Denis, neither of which still stands today.

The Sulpicians therefore decided to make a move to surpass their rivals once and for all. In 1823, to the great displeasure of local architects, they commissioned New York architect James O'Donnell, who came from an Irish Protestant background, to design the largest and most original church north of Mexico.

Basilique Notre-Dame ★★★, built between 1824 and 1829, is a true North-American masterpiece of Gothic Revival architecture. It should be seen not as a replica of a European cathedral, but rather as a fundamentally neoclassical structure characteristic of the Industrial Revolution, complemented by a medieval-style decor.

O'Donnell was so pleased with his work that he converted to Catholicism before his death, so that he could be buried under the church. Between 1874 and 1880, the original interior, considered too austere, was replaced by the fabulous polychromatic decorations found today. Executed by Victor Bourgeau, then the leading architect of religious buildings in the Montréal region, along with about 50 artists, it is made entirely of wood, painted and gilded with gold leaf.

Particularly noteworthy features include the baptistery, decorated with frescoes by Ozias Leduc, and the powerful electro-pneumatic Casavant organ with 7,000 pipes, often used during the numerous concerts given at the basilica. Lastly, there are the stained-glass windows by Francis Chigot, a master glass artist from France, which depict various episodes in the history of Montréal. They were installed in honour of the church's centennial.

To the right of the chancel, a passage leads to the Chapelle du Sacré-Cœur (Sacred Heart Chapel), added to the back of the church in 1888. Nicknamed *"Chapelle des Mariages"* (Wedding Chapel) because of the countless nuptials held there every year, it was seriously damaged by fire in 1978. The spiral staircases and the side galleries are all that remain of the exuberant, Spanish-style Gothic Revival decor of the original. The architects decided to tie in these vestiges with a modern design, completed in 1981, and included a lovely sectioned vault with skylights, a large bronze reredos by Charles Daudelin and a Guilbault-Thérien mechanical organ.

The **Vieux Séminaire Saint-Sulpice ★**, or old seminary, was built in 1683 in the style of a Parisian *hôtel particulier*, with a courtyard in front and a garden in back. It is the oldest building in the city. For more than three centuries, it has been occupied by Sulpician priests who, under the

Vieux-Montréal

The majestic Basilique Notre-Dame's interior, a masterpiece of Gothic Revival architecture in Old Montréal.
© Québec Religious Heritage Foundation

French Regime, used it as a manor from which they managed their vast seigneury. At the time of the building's construction, Montréal was home to barely 500 inhabitants and was constantly being terrorized by Iroquois attacks. Under those circumstances, the seminary, although modest in appearance, represented a precious haven of European civilization in the middle of the wilderness. The public clock at the top of the facade was installed in 1701, and may be the oldest one of its kind in the Americas.

The immense warehouses of the **Cours Le Royer** ★ belonged to the *religieuses hospitalières* (nursing sisters) of Saint-Joseph, who rented them out to importers. Designed between 1860 and 1871 by Michel Laurent and Victor Bourgeau, they are lo-

cated on the site of Montréal's first Hôtel-Dieu hospital, founded by Jeanne Mance in 1642. The warehouses, covering a total of 43,000m², were converted into apartments and offices between 1977 and 1986. The small Rue Le Royer was excavated to make room for an underground parking lot, now covered by a lovely pedestrian mall.

Old Montréal features a large number of 19th-century warehouses with stone frames used to store the goods unloaded from ships at the nearby port. Certain elements of their design—their large glass surfaces, intended to reduce the need for artificial gas lighting and consequently the risk of fire, their wide open interior spaces, the austere style of their Victorian facades— make these buildings the natural precursors of modern architecture. Many of the warehouses have been converted into hotels.

Drawn in 1672, **Rue Saint-Paul** ★ is Montréal's oldest street and long served as Montréal's main commercial artery. It is probably Old Montréal's most emblematic street, lined with 19th-century stone buildings that are home to art galleries, arts-and-crafts shops and jazz clubs, making it a great place for a stroll.

Montréal's oldest public square, **Place Royale**, dates back to 1657. Originally a market square, it later became a pretty Victorian garden surrounded by a cast-iron fence. In 1991, it was raised in order to make room for the archaeological crypt of the Pointe-à-Callière museum.

The **Maison de la Douane** is a lovely example of British neoclassical architecture transplanted into a Canadian setting. The old customs house was built in 1836 and is now an integral part of the Pointe-à-Callière museum.

Pointe-à-Callière, Musée d'Archéologie et d'Histoire de Montréal ★★ is an archaeology and history museum that lies on the exact site where Montréal was founded on May 17, 1642: **Pointe à Callière**. The Saint-Pierre river used to flow alongside the area now occupied by Place d'Youville, while the muddy banks of the St. Lawrence reached almost as far as the present-day Rue de la Commune. The first colonists built Fort Ville-Marie out of earth and wooden posts on the isolated point of land created by these two bodies of water. Threatened by Iroquois flotillas and flooding, the leaders of the colony soon decided to establish the town on Côteau Saint-Louis, the hill now bisected by Rue Notre-Dame. The site of the fort was then occupied by a cemetery and the château of Governor de Callière, hence the name.

The museum uses the most advanced technologies available to provide visitors with a survey of the city's history. Attractions include a multimedia presentation, a visit to

The gardens of the Vieux Séminaire Saint-Sulpice, built in 1683.
© MP-0000.10.104 / © McCord Museum of Canadian History

Vieux-Montréal

the vestiges discovered on the site, excellent models illustrating the stages of Place Royale's development, holograms and thematic exhibitions. The museum was established in 1992 to mark the city's 350th anniversary.

Stretching from Place Royale to Rue McGill, **Place d'Youville** owes its elongated shape to its location on top of the bed of the Rivière Saint-Pierre, which was canalized in 1832.

In the heart of Place d'Youville stands the former no. 3 fire station, one of Québec's rare examples of Flemish-inspired architecture. The station is now home to the **Centre d'Histoire de Montréal ★**. A lovely exhibit showcasing various objects relating Montréal's history is presented on the first floor. Thanks to lively presentations, visitors can follow the city's evolution and learn about significant events, such as Expo 67, discover daily life in various eras, hear about major strikes in the city and see how several heritage buildings were demolished. Sound effects, among other things, play a particularly important role here, as you can hear taped testimonies of Montrealers of various origins talking about their city. On the top floors are temporary exhibits, as well as a glass covered overpass from which you can admire Old Montréal.

Marché Sainte-Anne used to be located west of Rue Saint-Pierre and was the seat of the Province of Canada's Parliament from 1840 to 1849, when Orangemen burned the building down following the adoption of a compensatory law aimed at both English- and French-speaking victims of the 1837-1838 rebellions. This marked the end of Montréal's political vocation; Canada's Parliament was subsequently moved to Toronto, then Québec City and, finally, Ottawa in 1857.

Pointe-à-Callière, Montréal's museum of archaeology and history.
© Roderick Chen

Located on Place d'Youville, the Centre d'Histoire de Montréal occupies a former fire station.
© *Le Centre d'histoire de Montréal*

The Sœurs de la Charité (Sisters of Charity) are better known as the Sœurs Grises (Grey Nuns), a nickname given to these nuns who were falsely accused of selling alcohol to natives and getting them drunk (in French, *gris* means both grey and tipsy). In 1747, the founder of the community, Marguerite d'Youville, took charge of the former Hôpital des Frères Charon, established in 1693, and transformed it into the **Hôpital Général des Sœurs Grises** ★, a shelter for the city's homeless children. The west wing and the ruins of the chapel are all that remain of this complex, built during the 17th and 18th centuries in the shape of an *H*. The **Maison de Mère d'Youville**, which provides an overview of the life of the religious community's founder, can be visited here. The other part, which made up another of the old city's classical perspectives, was torn open when Rue Saint-Pierre was extended through the middle of the chapel. The right transept and part of the apse, visible on the right, have been reinforced in order to accommodate a work of art representing the text of the congregation's letters patent.

The former **Fonderie Darling** ★, located in what is now the Cité Multimédia, was converted into an arts centre thanks to an initiative by Quartier Éphémère, an organiza-

Vieux-Montréal

The former Fonderie Darling, now an arts centre, is located in Montréal's Cité Multimédia.
© Quartierephemere.org / Marie-Christine Abel

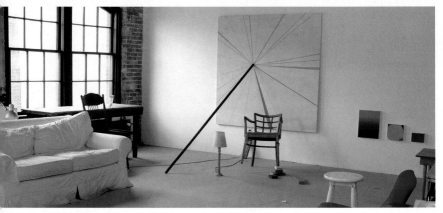

A Fonderie Darling artist's workshop.

© Quartierephemere.org / Félix Michaud

Vieux-Montréal

tion devoted to preserving the city's industrial heritage. Established in the industrial district in 1880, the foundry contributed to the development of Montréal's port. After being abandoned for many years, the building was renovated and is now a centre for the creation, production and promotion of works by young artists, and contains offices, art studios, a sound studio, an art gallery with an exhibit space and the Cluny ArtBar café-restaurant.

The **Cité Multimédia de Montréal ★** takes up a large chunk of the southwestern part of Old Montréal, i.e. the old Faubourg des Récollets. These buildings house several companies in the movie and multimedia industries, which brings a lot of life to a district that is now teeming with young workers all day long. The **Cognicase building ★** is definitely worth a look for its unique architecture.

The port of Montréal is the largest inland port on the continent. It stretches over 25km along the St. Lawrence River, from Cité du Havre to the refineries in the east end. The **Vieux-Port de Montréal / Old Port of Montréal** ★ corresponds to the historic portion of the port, located in front of the old city. Abandoned because of its obsolescence, it was revamped between 1983 and 1992, following the example of various other centrally located North-American ports. The old port encompasses a lovely park, laid out on the embankments and coupled with a promenade, which runs alongside the piers, or *quais*, offering a "window" on the river and the few shipping activities that have fortunately been maintained. The layout emphasizes the view of the water, the downtown area and Rue de la Commune, whose wall of neoclassical grey-stone warehouses stands before the city, one of the only examples of so-called "waterfront planning" in North America.

From the port, visitors can set off on an excursion on the river aboard the **Bateau-Mouche**, whose glass roof enables passengers to fully appreciate the beauty of the surroundings. The *navettes fluviales*, or river shuttles, ferry passengers to Île Sainte-Hélène and Longueuil, offering a spectacular view of the old port and Old Montréal along the way.

The **Lachine Canal** ★ was inaugurated in 1825. This waterway made it possible to bypass the formidable rapids known as the Rapides de Lachine, upriver from Montréal, thus providing access to the Great Lakes and the American Midwest. The canal also became the cradle of the industrial revolution in Canada since spinning and flour mills were able to harness its power, as well as a direct means of receiving supplies and sending out shipments. Closed in 1970, 11 years after the St. Lawrence Seaway was opened in 1959, the canal was turned over to the Canadian Parks Service. A

The Old Port's last great silos.

© iStockphoto.com / Tony Tremblay

Rue De La Commune and the downtown area, as seen from the Bassin Bonsecours.   © Stéphan Poulin

bicycle path now runs alongside it, continuing on to the Old Port. The locks lie adjacent to a park and a boldly designed lock-keeper's house. Nearby stands the last of the old port's towering **grain silos**. Erected in 1905, this reinforced concrete structure gained the admiration of architects Walter Gropius and Le Corbusier when they came here to study. It is now illuminated as if it were a monument. The port's **Gare Maritime Iberville** is the harbour station for the international cruise liners that pass through Montréal.

The **Centre des Sciences de Montréal**, an interactive science–and–entertainment complex set up on the King Edward pier, invites you to discover the secrets of the world of science and technology while having a great time. The centre features three exhibition halls where participants can enjoy science experiments, interactive games and several cultural and educational activities.

The **Auberge Saint-Gabriel** opened in 1754 and is the province's oldest still-operating inn. It occupies a group of 18th-century buildings with sturdy fieldstone walls.

The **Centre de Céramique Bonsecours**, a training, research, creation and promotion centre for ceramics in Québec, also houses an art gallery. It was founded about 20 years ago

in the former Caserne Saint-Gabriel, the oldest firehouse in Montréal that is still standing. This Victorian-style structure was built in 1871-1872.

No fewer than three courthouses are found along Rue Notre-Dame. Inaugurated in 1971, the massive new **Palais de Justice**, or courthouse, dwarfs the surroundings. A sculpture by Charles Daudelin entitled *Allegrocube* stands on its steps. A mechanism makes it possible to open and close this stylized "hand of justice."

From the time it was inaugurated in 1926 until it closed in 1970, the **Édifice Ernest-Cormier ★★** was used for criminal proceedings. The former courthouse was converted into a conservatory and was named after

its architect, the illustrious Ernest Cormier, who also designed the main pavilion of the Université de Montréal and the doors of the United Nations Headquarters in New York City. The Édifice Ernest-Cormier returned to its original use in 2004, as the seat of the Québec Court of Appeal. The courthouse is graced with outstanding bronze sconces, cast in Paris at the workshops of Edgar Brandt. Their installation in 1925 ushered in the Art Deco style in Canada. The main hall, faced with travertine and topped by three dome-shaped skylights, is worth a quick visit.

The former **Palais de Justice ★**, the oldest courthouse in Montréal, was built between 1849 and 1856 on the site of the first courthouse, which

Place Jacques-Cartier and, in the background, the Colonne Nelson.   © *Dreamstime.com*

Vieux-Montréal

was erected in 1800. It is another fine example of Canadian neoclassical architecture. After the courts were divided in 1926, the old Palais was used for civil cases, judged according to the Napoleonic Code. Since the opening of the new courthouse, the old Palais has been converted into an annex of the neighbouring City Hall.

Place Jacques-Cartier ★ was laid out on the site once occupied by the Château de Vaudreuil, which burned down in 1803. The former Montréal residence of the governor of New France was without question the most elegant private home in the city. Designed by engineer Gaspard Chaussegros de Léry in 1723, it had a horseshoe-shaped staircase leading up to a handsome cut-stone portal, two projecting pavilions (one on each side of the main part of the building), and a formal garden that extended as far as Rue Notre-Dame. After the fire, the property was purchased by lo-

cal merchants, who decided to give the government a small strip of land, on the condition that a public market be established there, thus increasing the value of the adjacent property that remained in private hands. This explains Place Jacques-Cartier's oblong shape.

Merchants of British descent sought various means of ensuring their visibility and publicly expressing their patriotism in Montréal. They quickly formed a much larger community in Montréal than in Québec City, where government and military headquarters were located. In 1809, they were the first in the world to erect a monument to Admiral Horatio Nelson, who defeated the combined French and Spanish fleets in the Battle of Trafalgar. Supposedly, they even got French-Canadian merchants drunk in order to extort a financial contribution from them for the project. The base of the **Colonne Nelson**, or Nelson Column, was designed and executed

SPOTLIGHT ON THE CITY

Since 1996, Old Montréal has featured a lighting plan whose goal is to showcase the beauty of its old buildings and monuments at night to make them even more stunning. Thanks to well-designed lighting systems, facades and statues come out of the shadows and reveal architectural or sculptural facets that are often imperceptible by daylight.

Old Montréal's lighting plan has become the envy of the city's other boroughs, who also want to highlight their architectural heritage and works of public art. In 2005, the City inaugurated its first lighting project outside of Old Montréal: the Maison Saint-Gabriel, a historic site located in the Sud-Ouest borough, in Pointe Saint-Charles.

Old Montréal by night.

in London. It is decorated with bas-relief depicting the exploits of the famous admiral at Abukir, Copenhagen and, of course, Trafalgar. The statue of Nelson at the top was originally made of an artificial type of stone, but after being damaged time and time again by protestors, it was finally replaced by a fibre-glass replica in 1981. The column is the oldest extant monument in Montréal.

At the other end of Place Jacques-Cartier is the **Quai Jacques-Cartier** and the river, while **Rue Saint-Amable** lies tucked away at the halfway mark. In summer, artists and artisans gather on this little street, selling jewellery, drawings, etchings and caricatures.

Under the French Regime, Montréal, following the example of Québec City and Trois-Rivières, had its own governor, not to be confused with the governor of New France. The situation was the same under the

English Regime. It wasn't until 1833 that the first elected mayor, Jacques Viger, took control of the city. This man, who was passionate about history, gave Montréal its motto (*Concordia Salus*) and coat of arms, composed of the four symbols of the "founding" peoples, namely the French *fleur de lys*, the Irish clover, the Scottish thistle and the English rose, all linked together by the Canadian beaver.

After occupying a number of inadequate buildings for decades, the municipal administration finally moved into its present home in 1878. The **Hôtel de Ville ★ ★**, or city hall, a fine example of the Second Empire, or Napoleon III, style, is the work of Henri-Maurice Perrault, who also designed the neighbouring courthouse. In 1922, a fire destroyed the interior and roof of the building which was later restored in 1926 on the model of the city hall in Tours, France. Exhibitions are occasionally presented in the main hall, which is accessible via the main entrance. It was from the balcony of this building that France's General de Gaulle cried out his famous *"Vive le Québec libre!"* ("Long live a free Québec!") in 1967, to the great delight of the crowd gathered in front of the building.

The statue of Admiral Jean Vauquelin (1728-1772), defender of Louisbourg at the end of the French Regime, was probably put here in 1930 to counterbalance the monument to Nelson, a symbol of British control over Canada. From **Place Vauquelin**, a staircase leads to the **Champ-de-Mars**, which was modified in 1991 in order to reveal some vestiges of the fortifications that once surrounded

Montréal's City Hall, a fine example of Second Empire architecture.
© Dreamstime.com

The Château Ramezay was built for the Governor of Montréal in 1705.   © Château Ramezay Museum

Montréal. Gaspard Chaussegros de Léry designed Montréal's ramparts, erected between 1717 and 1745, as well as those of Québec City. The walls of Montréal, however, never lived through war, as the city's commercial calling and location ruled out such rash acts. The large, tree-lined lawns are reminders of the Champ-de-Mars' former vocation as a parade ground for military manoeuvres until 1924. A view of the downtown area's skyscrapers opens up through the clearing.

Facing City Hall is the beautiful **Place De La Dauversière ★**, home to several works of public art, notably the statue of one of Montréal's former mayors, Jean Drapeau. A very popular mayor, Mr. Drapeau reigned over "his" city for nearly 30 years.

The **Château Ramezay Museum ★★** is located in the humblest of all the "châteaux" built in Montréal, and the only one still standing. Château Ramezay was built in 1705 for the governor of Montréal, Claude de Ramezay, and his family. In 1745, it fell into the hands of the Compagnie des Indes Occidentales (The French West Indies Company), which made it its North-American headquarters. Precious Canadian furs were stored in its vaults awaiting shipment to France. After the conquest, the British occupied the house, before being temporarily removed by American insurgents who wanted Québec to join the nascent United States. Benjamin Franklin even came to stay at the château for a few months in 1775, in an attempt to convince Montrealers to become American citizens.

Vieux-Montréal

Vibrant nightlife on Place Jacques-Cartier.   © Stéphan Poulin

In 1895, after serving as the first building of the Montréal branch of the Université Laval in Québec City, the château was converted into a museum, under the patronage of the Société d'Archéologie et de Numismatique de Montréal, founded by Jacques Viger. Château Ramezay boasts a rich collection of furniture, clothing and everyday objects from the 18th and 19th centuries, as well as many Aboriginal artifacts. The Salle de Nantes is decorated with beautiful Louis XV-style mahogany panelling, designed by Germain Boffrand and imported from the Nantes office of the Compagnie des Indes (circa 1725).

In addition, Château Ramezay features a pretty indoor green space, the "neo-formal" Jardin du Gouverneur garden, as well as the Café du Château and the Marie-Charlotte shop.

The **Sir George-Étienne-Cartier National Historic Site ★** consists of twin houses that were successively inhabited by George-Étienne Cartier, one of the Fathers of Canadian Confederation. Inside, visitors will find a reconstructed mid-19th-century French-Canadian bourgeois home. Interesting educational soundtracks accompany the tour and add a touch of authenticity to the site.

THE ST. LAWRENCE RIVER

On August 10, 1535, feast day of patron Saint Lawrence, Jacques Cartier ventured inland for the first time on a great river. He found himself in the Côte-Nord region and named a bay after the deacon: *baye sainct Laurens*. A few years later, Spanish or Italian navigators made things more confusing by giving the same name to the gulf. In 1569, the publication of the famous Mercator map became the final step in naming the entire river, and not only the gulf, "Saint-Laurent."

When Samuel de Champlain referred to the waterway between the St. John River (New Brunswick) and the St. Lawrence River via Lake Témiscouata in his writings, he already used the name: *"In 1604, Ralleau, secretary of Sieur de Mons, learned from Secondon, chief of said river, that the country's inhabitants travel on this river all the way to Tadoussac, which is in the great St. Lawrence River, and pass over only little land to get there."* This new name eventually replaced all older appellations, which included "great walking road," "great river of Hochelaga," "great river of Canada" and "river of Canada."

Sailing up the St. Lawrence in 1535, Jacques Cartier was forced to stop by what are now know as the Lachine Rapids, which made it impossible to go any further. To bypass this obstacle, the Lachine Canal was opened in 1825 and operated until 1970, the St. Lawrence Seaway having already taken over since 1959.

A sculpted angel looks out onto the St. Lawrence River from the top of the Chapelle Notre-Dame-de-Bon-Secours.
© Productions Train d'enfer

The neighbouring building is the former **Cathédrale Schismatique Grecque Saint-Nicolas**, built around 1910 in the Romanesque-Byzantine Revival style.

Rue Berri marks the eastern border of Old Montréal, and thus the fortified city of the French Regime, beyond which extended the Faubourg Québec, excavated in the 19th century to make way for railroad lines. This explains the sharp difference in height between the hill known as Côteau Saint-Louis and the Viger and Dalhousie stations.

Gare Viger was inaugurated by Canadian Pacific in 1897 in order to serve the eastern part of the country. Its resemblance to the Château Frontenac in Québec City is not a coincidence; both buildings were designed for the same railroad company and by the same architect, an American named Bruce Price. The Château-style station, which closed in 1935, also included a prestigious hotel and large stained-glass train shed that has since been destroyed.

The small **Gare Dalhousie** was the first railway station built by Canadian Pacific, a company established for the purpose of building a Canadian transcontinental railroad. The station was the starting point of the first transcontinental train headed for Port Moody (20km from Van-

Maison Pierre du Calvet is typical of 18th-century French urban architecture. © Gaëtan Trottier

couver) on June 28, 1886. It is now home to the Éloize circus company.

The port's former refrigerated warehouse, made of brown brick, and Île Sainte-Hélène, in the middle of the river, can both be seen from the Rue Notre-Dame overpass. The island, along with Île Notre-Dame, was the site of Expo 67.

A chapel was built in 1658 under the orders of Marguerite Bourgeoys, founder of the congregation of Notre-Dame, on the site of the present **Chapelle Notre-Dame-de-Bon-Secours ★**, which dates back to 1771, when the Sulpicians wanted to establish a branch of the main parish in the eastern part of the fortified city. In 1890, the chapel

was modified to suit contemporary tastes, and the present stone facade was added, along with the "aerial" chapel (1893-1894) that looks out on the port. Parishioners asked for God's blessing on ships and crews bound for Europe from this chapel. The interior, redone at the same time, contains a large number of votive offerings from sailors saved from shipwrecks. Some are in the form of model ships, hung from the ceiling of the nave.

Between 1996 and 1998, excavations below the chapel's nave uncovered several artifacts, including some dating from the colony's early days. Today, the **Musée Marguerite-Bourgeoys ★** displays these interesting archaeological finds. But there is even more to explore: adjoining the Notre-Dame-de-Bon-Secours chapel, it leads from the top of the tower, where the view is breathtaking, to the depths of the crypt, where the old stones tell their own story. Learn about the life of Marguerite Bourgeoys, a pioneer of education in Québec, admire her portrait and discover the mystery surrounding her. Guided tours of the archaeological site surrounding the foundations of the stone chapel, the oldest in Montréal, are offered.

The **Maison Pierre du Calvet** was built in 1725 and is representative of 18th-century French urban architecture adapted to the local setting, with thick walls made of fieldstone embedded in mortar, storm windows doubling the casement windows with their little squares of glass imported from France, and high firebreak walls, then required by local regulations as a means of limiting the spread of fire from one building to the next. One of Montréal's best inns has been located in the house

Vieux-Montréal

for many years: **Hostellerie Pierre du Calvet** and its restaurant, **Les Filles du Roy**.

A little higher on Rue Bonsecours, visitors will find the **Maison Papineau** inhabited long ago by Louis-Joseph Papineau (1786-1871), lawyer, politician and head of the French-Canadian nationalist movement until the insurrection of 1837. Built in 1785 and covered with a wooden facing made to look like cut stone, it was one of the first buildings in Old Montréal to be restored (1962).

The **Marché Bonsecours** ★★ was erected between 1845 and 1850. The lovely grey-stone neoclassical edifice with sash windows is located between Rue Saint-Paul and Rue de la Commune. The building is adorned with a portico supported by cast-iron columns moulded in England, and topped by a silvery dome, which for many years served as the symbol of the city at the entrance to the port. The public market, closed in the early 1960s following the advent of the supermarket, was transformed into municipal offices, then an exhibition hall before finally partially reopening in 1996. The market now presents an exhibition and features arts-and-crafts shops. The market's old storehouses can be seen on Rue Saint-Paul. From the large balcony

on Rue de la Commune, you can see the partially reconstructed Bonsecours dock, where paddle-wheelers, full of farmers who came to the city to sell their produce, used to moor.

The pale yellow **Tour de l'Horloge** ★ is actually a monument that was erected in 1922 in memory of merchant marine sailors who died during WWI. It was inaugurated by the Prince of Wales (who be-

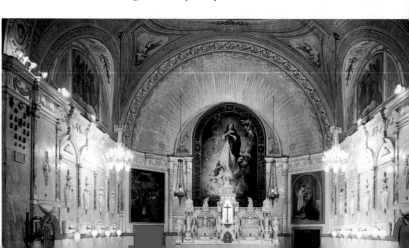

Rue De La Commune and the neoclassical Marché Bonsecours.
© iStockphoto.com / Tony Tremblay

came King Edward VIII) during one of his many visits to Montréal. An observatory at the top of the tower provides a clear view of Île Sainte-Hélène, the Jacques-Cartier bridge and the eastern part of Old Montréal. At the base of the tower, one has the impression of standing on the deck of a ship as it glides slowly down the St. Lawrence and out to the Atlantic Ocean.

The Chapelle Notre-Dame-de-Bon-Secours choir.
© Normand Rajotte

A view of the Quai de l'Horloge from the Chapelle Notre-Dame-de-Bon-Secours lookout.
© Productions Train d'enfer

Vieux-Montréal

Île Sainte-Hélène and Île Notre-Dame

The Biosphère by night.

When Samuel de Champlain crossed the island of Montréal from the Rivière des Prairies to the "Place Royale" in 1611, he found a small rocky archipelago facing the isle. He named the largest of these islands after his wife, Hélène Boulé. Île Sainte-Hélène later became part of the seigneury of Longueuil. In 1760, the island was the last foothold of French troops in New France, commanded by Chevalier François de Lévis.

In the early 1960s, Montréal was chosen as the site of the 1967 World's Fair (Expo 67). The city wanted to set up the event on a large, attractive site near the downtown area; such a site, however, did not exist. So it became necessary to build one: using soil excavated during the construction of the metro tunnel, Île Notre-Dame was created, doubling the area of Île Sainte-Hélène. From April to November 1967, 45 million visitors passed through Cité du Havre, the gateway to the fairground, and criss-crossed both islands. Expo, as Montrealers still refer to it, was more than a jumble of assorted objects; it was Montréal's awakening, during which the city opened itself to the world, and visitors from all over discovered a new art of living.

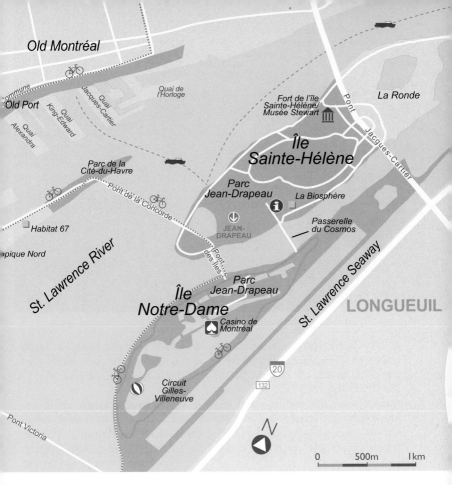

Old Montréal

Old Port

Quai de l'Horloge

Fort de l'île Sainte-Hélène/ Musée Stewart

La Ronde

Pont Jacques-Cartier

Île Sainte-Hélène

Quai Alexandra

Quai King-Edward

Quai Jacques-Cartier

Parc de la Cité-du-Havre

Pont de la Concorde

Habitat 67

pique Nord

Parc Jean-Drapeau

La Biosphère

JEAN-DRAPEAU

Passerelle du Cosmos

St. Lawrence River

Pont des Îles

Île Notre-Dame

Parc Jean-Drapeau

St. Lawrence Seaway

LONGUEUIL

Casino de Montréal

Circuit Gilles-Villeneuve

20

132

Pont Victoria

0   500m   1 km

Tropique Nord ★ , Habitat 67 ★ ★ and **Parc de la Cité-du-Havre ★** were all built on a spit of land created to protect the port of Montréal from ice and currents. This site also offers lovely views of the city and the water. A little further is the large glass wall of Tropique Nord, a residential complex composed of apartments with a view of the outdoors on one side and an interior tropical garden on the other.

Next is Habitat 67, an experimental housing development that was built for Expo 67 in order to highlight new construction techniques using prefabricated concrete slabs, and to herald a new art of living. Its architect, Moshe Safdie, was only 23 years old when he drew up the plans for this strange structure.

At Parc de la Cité-du-Havre, visitors will find 12 panels containing a brief description of the history of the St. Lawrence River. A section of the bicycle path leading to Île Notre-Dame and Île Sainte-Hélène passes through the park.

Parc Jean-Drapeau ★ ★ encompasses Île Notre-Dame and Île Sainte-Hélène. The latter originally covered an area of 50ha but was enlarged to over 120ha for Expo 67. The original portion corresponds to the raised area studded with breccia boulders. Peculiar to this island, breccia is

Habitat 67's strange cluster of concrete cubes.

a very hard, ferrous stone that takes on an orange colour when exposed to air for a long time. In 1992, the western part was transformed into a vast open-air amphitheatre where large-scale shows are presented. In this lovely riverside park, visitors will find *L'Homme* (*Man*), a large metal sculpture by Alexander Calder, created for Expo 67.

A work by Mexican artist Sebastián entitled *La Porte de l'Amitié* (The Door to Friendship) can be found on Île Sainte-Hélène. This sculpture was given to the

Île Sainte-Hélène and Île Notre-Dame

The military manoeuvres of the Compagnie Franche de la Marine are brought to life at the Fort de l'Île Sainte-Hélène.
© Musée Stewart

City of Montréal by Mexico City in 1992 and erected on this site three years later to commemorate the signing of the free-trade agreement between Canada, the United States and Mexico (NAFTA).

The pool house, with a facade of breccia stone, and outdoor swimming pools, built during the Great Depression, lie at the edge of the original park. The island's three original pools were taken apart and then rebuilt for the 2005 FINA World Aquatic Championships. The island, with its varied contours, is dominated by the **Tour de Lévis**, a simple water tower built in 1936 that looks like a dungeon.

After the War of 1812 between the United States and Great Britain, the **Fort de l'Île Sainte-Hélène** ★ ★ was built so that Montréal could be properly defended. Its construction was completed in 1825. Built of breccia stone, the fort is in the shape of a jagged *U*, surrounding a drill ground used today by the Compagnie Franche de la Marine and the 78th Regiment of the Fraser Highlanders

Île Notre-Dame, Île Sainte-Hélène and the Biosphère environmental museum.   © Philippe Renault

The International des Feux Loto-Québec fireworks competition lights up the sky at La Ronde.
© La Ronde

Île Sainte-Hélène and Île Notre-Dame

as a parade ground. These two costumed mock regiments delight visitors by reviving Canada's French and Scottish military traditions. The drill ground also offers a lovely view of both the port and Pont Jacques-Cartier, which was inaugurated in 1930.

The fort's arsenal is now occupied by the **Musée Stewart ★★**, which is dedicated to colonial history and the exploration of the New World. The museum exhibits objects from past centuries, including interesting collections of maps, firearms, and scientific and navigational instruments collected by Montréal industrialist David Stewart and his wife Liliane.

La Ronde ★, an amusement park set up for Expo 67 on the former Île Ronde, opens its doors to both the young and the not-so-young every summer. The **L'International des Feux Loto-Québec** international fireworks competition is held here during the months of June and July.

Built in 1938 as a sports pavilion, **Restaurant Hélène de Champlain ★** was inspired by the architecture of New France and is reminiscent of the summer house of the Barony of Longueuil, once located in the area. Behind the restaurant is a lovely rose garden planted for Expo 67, which embellishes the view from the dining room. The **former military cemetery** of the British garrison stationed on Île Sainte-Hélène from 1828 to 1870 lies in front of the building. Most of the original tombstones have disappeared; a commemorative monument, erected in 1937, stands in their place.

The **Biosphère** ★ ★, built of tubular aluminum and measuring 80m in diameter, unfortunately lost its translucent acrylic skin in a fire back in 1976. Since 1995, it has housed a museum which showcases environmental issues related to water, climate changes, the Great Lakes – St. Lawrence River ecosystem, sustainable development and responsible consumption.

Île Notre-Dame emerged from the waters of the St. Lawrence in just 10 months, with the help of 15 million tons of rock and soil transported here from the metro construction site. Because it is an artificial island, its engineers and architects were able to give it a fanciful form by shaping both the soil and water. The island is traversed by charming **canals** and **gardens** ★ ★, laid out for the 1980 Floralies Internationales, an international flower show.

The main building of the **Casino de Montréal** ★ is housed in the aluminum structure of the old **French Pavilion** ★ on Île Notre-Dame. The upper galleries offer some lovely views of downtown Montréal and the St. Lawrence Seaway. Nearby is the former **Québec Pavilion** ★, shaped like a truncated pyramid.

The dazzling waterfront location of the Casino de Montréal. © iStockphoto.com / Tony Tremblay

Île Notre-Dame's Circuit Gilles-Villeneuve hosts the Grand Prix of Canada every year.
© Grand Prix of Canada-Brousseau

Île Sainte-Hélène and Île Notre-Dame

Nearby, visitors will find the entrance to the **Plage de l'Île Notre-Dame**, a beach enabling Montrealers to lounge on real sand right in the middle of the St. Lawrence. A natural filtering system keeps the water in the small lake clean, with no need for chemical additives. The number of swimmers allowed on the beach is strictly regulated, however, so as not to disrupt the balance of the system.

There are other recreational facilities here as well, namely the **Olympic Basin**, created for the rowing competitions of the 1976 Olympics, and the **Circuit Gilles-Villeneuve**, where Formula One drivers compete every year in the Grand Prix du Canada, part of the famous international racing competition.

Downtown

Downtown skyscrapers give Montréal a typically North-American look. Nevertheless, unlike most other cities on the continent, there is a certain Latin spirit here, which seeps in between the towering buildings, enlivening this part of Montréal both day and night. Bars, cafés, department stores, shops and corporate head offices, along with two universities and numerous colleges, all lie clustered within a limited area at the foot of Mount Royal.

The city centre underwent a radical transformation in a very short time (1960-1967), which included the construction of Place Ville Marie, the metro, the underground city, Place des Arts and various other infrastructures that still exert an influence on the area's development.

© Philippe Renault

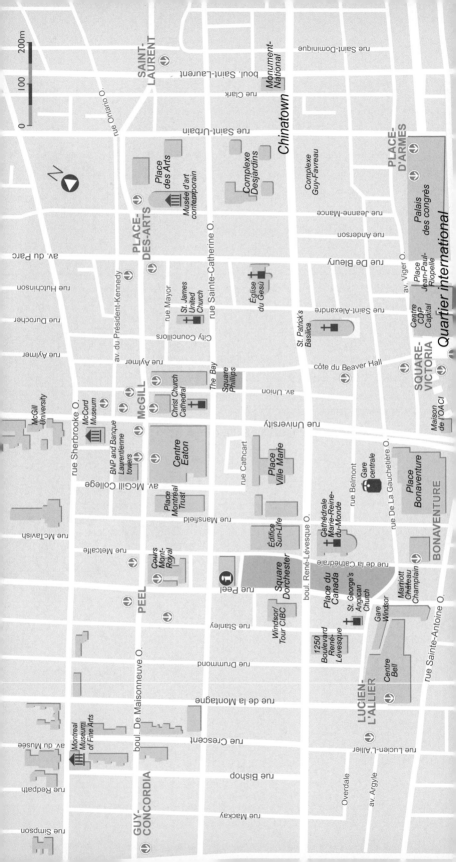

Red dots of light show the way along the Quartier des Spectacles' sidewalks at night.
© Martine Doyon – Quartier des spectacles

Montréal has the most extensive **indoor pedestrian network ★** (sometimes referred to as "underground Montréal") in the world. Greatly appreciated in bad weather, it covers some 30km and provides access, via various tunnels, atriums and plazas, to more than 2,000 shops and restaurants, as well as movie theatres, apartment and office buildings, hotels, parking lots, and bus and train stations.

The **Cours Mont-Royal ★★** are linked to this sprawling network, which centres around the various metro stations. A multi-purpose complex, Les Cours consists of four levels of stores, offices and

THE INDOOR PEDESTRIAN NETWORK

The construction of Place Ville Marie in 1962, with its basement shopping mall, marked the start of what is now known as the city's "Indoor Pedestrian Network." The development of this "city under the city" was hastened by the construction of the metro, which began in 1962. Within a short time, many of the downtown area's main businesses, office buildings and hotels were strategically linked to the underground pedestrian network and, by extension, the metro.

Today, five main areas make up what has now become the world's largest underground city.

- Around the Berri-UQAM station, providing access to the Université du Québec à Montréal (UQAM) buildings, Place Dupuis, the Grande Bibliothèque and the Station Centrale bus station.

- Between the Place-des-Arts and Place-d'Armes stations, providing access to Place des Arts, the Musée d'Art Contemporain, Complexe Desjardins, Complexe Guy-Favreau and the Palais des Congrès.

- Beneath the business district that surrounds the Square-Victoria metro station.

- Around the McGill, Peel and Bonaventure metro stations. It includes shopping malls and department stores like La Baie (The Bay) and Centre Eaton.

- In the commercial sector that surrounds the Atwater metro station and neighbouring Westmount Square and Place Alexis Nihon.

The Square-Victoria metro station's vast minimalist passageway.

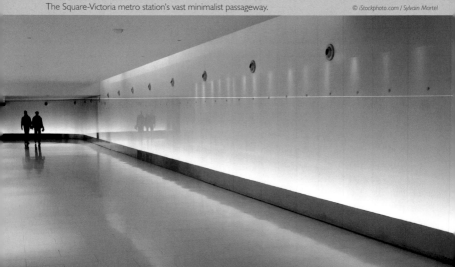

The deforming prism of Montréal's downtown skyscrapers.

apartments laid out inside the former Mount Royal Hotel. With its 1,100 rooms, this Jazz Age palace, inaugurated in 1922, was the largest hotel in the British Empire. Aside from the exterior, all that was preserved during the 1987 remodelling was a portion of the lobby's ceiling, from which the former chandelier of the Monte Carlo casino is suspended. The four 10-storey *cours* (inner courts) are definitely worth a visit, as is a stroll through what may be the best-designed shopping centre in the downtown area. The building that looks like a small Scottish manor across the street is the head office of the Seagram distillery.

From 1799 to 1854, **Square Dorchester ★** was occupied by Montréal's Catholic cemetery, which was later moved to Mount Royal, where it is still located. In 1872, the city turned the free space into two squares, one on either side of Dorchester Street (now Boulevard René-Lévesque). The northern portion is called Square Dorchester, while the southern part was renamed Place du Canada to commemorate the 100th anniversary of Confederation (1967). A number of monuments adorn Square Dorchester. In the centre is an equestrian statue dedicated to Canadian soldiers who died during the Boer War in South Africa, while around the perimeter stand a handsome

Downtown

The Édifice Sun Life, adorned with imposing colonnades, is where the British Crown Jewels were kept during World War II.
© Stéphan Poulin

statue of Scottish poet Robert Burns, styled after Bartholdi's *The Lion of Belfort* and donated by the Sun Life insurance company, and Émile Brunet's monument to Sir Wilfrid Laurier, Prime Minister of Canada from 1896 to 1911. The square also serves as the starting point for guided bus tours.

Le Windsor ★, the hotel where members of the royal family used to stay during their visits to Canada, no longer exists. All that remains is an annex erected in 1906, which was converted into an of-fice building in 1986. The ball-rooms and lovely Peacock Alley have, however, been preserved. An impressive atrium, visible from the upper floors, has been constructed for the building's tenants. The handsome **Tour CIBC** stands on the site of the old hotel. Its walls are faced with green slate, which blends harmoniously with the dominant colours of the buildings around the square, the greyish beige of stone and the green of oxidized copper.

The **Édifice Sun Life** ★★, erected between 1913 and 1933 for the powerful Sun Life insurance company, was for many years the largest building in the British Empire. It was in this "fortress" of the Anglo-Saxon establishment, with its colonnades reminiscent of ancient mythology, that the British Crown Jewels were hidden during World War II. In 1977, the company's head office was moved to Toronto, in protest against provincial language laws excluding English. Fortunately, the chimes that ring at 5pm every day are still in place and remain an integral part of the neighbourhood's spirit.

Place du Canada ★, the southern portion of Square Dorchester, is the setting for the annual Remembrance Day ceremony (November 11th), which honours Canadian soldiers killed in the two World Wars and the Korean War. Veterans reunite around the War Memorial, which occupies the place of honour in the centre of the square. A more imposing monument to Sir John A. Macdonald, Canada's first Prime Minister, elected in 1867, stands alongside Boulevard René-Lévesque.

A number of churches were clustered around Square Dorchester before it was even laid out in 1872. Unfortunately, only two of the eight churches built in the area between 1865 and 1875 have survived. One of these is **Cathédrale Marie-Reine-du-Monde** ★★, the seat of the archdiocese of Montréal and a reminder of the tremendous power wielded by the clergy up

St. George's Anglican Church boasts a magnificent Gothic Revival-style sculpted sandstone exterior.
© Shutterstock

Night lights provide an enchanting view of the Cathédrale Marie-Reine-du-Monde's pale-green facade.
© Stéphan Poulin

until the Quiet Revolution. It is exactly one third the size of St. Peter's in Rome.

In 1852, a terrible fire destroyed the Catholic cathedral on Rue Saint-Denis, so the ambitious Monseigneur Ignace Bourget (1799-1885), who was bishop of Montréal at the time, seized the opportunity to work out a grandiose scheme to outshine the Sulpicians' Basilique Notre-Dame and ensure the supremacy of the Catholic Church in Montréal. What could accomplish this better than a replica of Rome's St. Peter's, right in the middle of the Protestant neighbourhood? Despite reservations on the part of architect

Victor Bourgeau, the plan was carried out. The bishop even sent Bourgeau to Rome to measure the venerable building. Construction began in 1870 and was finally completed in 1894. The copper statues of the 13 patron saints of Montréal's parishes were installed in 1900.

Modernized during the 1950s, the interior of the cathedral is no longer as harmonious as it once was. Nevertheless, there is a lovely replica of Bernini's baldaquin, executed by sculptor Victor Vincent. The bishops and archbishops of Montréal are interred in the mortuary chapel, where the place of honour is occupied by the recumbent statue of Monseigneur Bourget. An outdoor monument reminds visitors of this individual, who did so much to strengthen the bonds between France and Canada.

The beautiful Gothic Revival–style **St. George's Anglican Church**'s ★★ delicately sculpted sandstone ex-terior conceals an interior covered with lovely, dark woodwork. Particularly noteworthy are the remarkable ceiling, with its exposed framework, the woodwork in the chancel and the tapestry from Westminster Abbey, used during the coronation of Queen Elizabeth II.

The elegant 47-storey **1250 Boulevard René-Lévesque ★** building neighbours St. George's Anglican Church and was completed in 1991. Its winter bamboo garden is open to the public.

In 1887, the head of Canadian Pacific, William Cornelius Van Horne, asked his New York friend Bruce Price (1845-1903) to draw up plans for **Gare Windsor / Windsor Station ★★**, a modern train station that would serve as the railroad company's headquarters. At the time, Price was one of the most prominent architects in the eastern United States, where he worked on residential projects for high-society clients, as well as

Montréal's most splendid example of Romanesque Revival architecture, Windsor Station. © iStockphoto.com/Anneclaire

skyscrapers like the American Surety Building in Manhattan. Later, he was put in charge of building the Château Frontenac in Québec City, thus establishing the Château style in Canada.

The massive-looking Gare Windsor, with its corner buttresses, Roman arches outlined in stone and series of arcades, is Montréal's best example of the Romanesque Revival style. Its construction established the city as the country's railway centre. Abandoned in favour of the Gare Centrale after World War II, Windsor Station was used only for commuter trains up until 1993. Today, the Gare Windsor houses many stores and offices, and its waiting hall is used for various events.

The **Centre Bell**, built on the platforms of Windsor Station, now blocks all train access to the venerable old station. Opened in 1996, this immense, oddly shaped building succeeds the Forum on Rue Sainte-Catherine as the home of the National Hockey League's famous **Montréal Canadiens**. During a game, the place is packed and vibrant.

Built in 1966, the **Château Champlain ★**, nicknamed the "cheese grater" by Montrealers due to its many arched, convex openings, was designed by Québec architects Jean-Paul Pothier and Roger D'Astous.

The **Planétarium de Montréal ★** projects astronomy films onto a 20m hemispheric dome. The universe and its mysteries are explained in a way that makes this marvellous, often poorly understood world accessible to all.

The universe reveals its secrets at the Planétarium de Montréal. © Planétarium de Montréal

The Montréal Canadiens play their home games at the Centre Bell.

An immense, grooved concrete block with no facade, **Place Bonaventure ★**, which was completed in 1966, is one of the most revolutionary works of modern architecture of its time. Designed by Montrealer Raymond Affleck, it is a multi-purpose complex built on top of the railway lines leading to the Gare Centrale. It contains a parking area, a bi-level shopping centre linked to the metro and the underground city, two large exhibition halls, wholesalers, offices and an intimate 400-room hotel laid out around a charming hanging garden, worth a short visit.

A railway tunnel below Mount Royal linked to the downtown area was built in 1913. The tracks ran under Avenue McGill College, then multiplied at the bottom of a deep trench, which stretched between Rue Mansfield and Rue University. In 1938, the subterranean **Gare Centrale** was built for the Canadien National railroad company, marking the true starting point of the underground city.

Downtown

Place Ville Marie undergoing construction during the early 1960s.

© Courtesy of Place Ville Marie

Downtown

Partly hidden since 1957 by the Hôtel Reine-Elizabeth, it has an interesting, streamlined Art Deco waiting hall.

Place Ville Marie ★ ★ ★ was erected above the northern part of the former open-air trench in 1962. Famous Chinese-American architect I.M. Pei (Louvre Pyramid, Paris; East Building of the National Gallery of Art, Washington, DC) designed the multi-purpose complex built over the railway tracks and containing vast shopping arcades now linked to most of the surrounding edifices. It also encompasses a number of office buildings, including the famous cruciform aluminum tower, whose unusual shape enables natural light to penetrate all the way into the centre of the structure, while at the same time symbolizing Montréal, a Catholic city dedicated to the Virgin Mary.

Avenue McGill College ★ was still a narrow residential street in 1950. It now offers a wide view of Mount Royal and its crowning metal cross.

The twin **BNP and Banque Laurentienne towers ★**, certainly the best designed buildings on Avenue McGill College, were built in 1981. Their bluish glass walls set off a sculpture entitled *La Foule Illuminée* (The Illuminated Crowd), by Franco-British artist Raymond Mason.

Rue Sainte-Catherine is Montréal's main commercial artery. It stretches along 15km, changing in appearance several times along the way. Around 1870, it was still lined with row houses; by 1920, however, it had already become an integral part of life in Montréal. Since the 1960s, a number of shopping centres linking the street to the adjacent metro lines have sprouted up among the local businesses. The **Centre Eaton** is the most recent of these. It is composed of a long, old-fashioned gallery lined with five levels of shops and restaurants, and is linked to Place Ville Marie by a pedestrian tunnel.

The **Eaton** department store, one of the largest department stores on Rue Sainte-Catherine and an institution across Canada, went bankrupt in 1999 and had to close its doors. Its magnificent Art Deco dining room on the ninth floor, designed by Jacques Carlu and completed in 1931, is a historic monument, but is not currently open to the public.

The first Anglican cathedral in Montréal stood on Rue Notre-Dame, not far from Place d'Armes.

Place Ville Marie was designed by architect Ieoh Ming Pei, who also created the Louvre Pyramid in Paris.
© Courtesy of Place Ville Marie

The Christ Church Cathedral now stands on the roof of a shopping centre.

© Philippe Renault

After a fire in 1856, **Christ Church Cathedral ★★** was relocated to be closer to the community it served. Using the cathedral of his hometown, Salisbury, as his model, architect Frank Wills designed a flamboyant structure, with a single steeple rising above the transepts. The plain interior contrasts with the rich ornamentation of the Catholic churches of the area. A few beautiful stained-glass windows from the workshops of William Morris provide the only bit of colour. The steeple's stone spire was destroyed in 1927 and replaced by an aluminum replica; otherwise, it would have eventually caused the building to sink. The problem, linked to the instability of the foundation, was not resolved, however, until a shopping centre, the **Promenades de la Cathédrale**, was constructed under the building in 1987. Christ Church Anglican Cathedral thus rests on the roof of the mall. At the same time, a postmodern glass skyscraper topped by a "crown of thorns" was erected behind the cathedral. At its base is a little garden that honours architect Raoul

Wallenberg, a Swedish diplomat who saved several Hungarian Jews from Nazi deportation during the Second World War.

It was around **Square Phillips** ★ that the first stores appeared along Rue Sainte-Catherine, which was once strictly residential. Henry Morgan moved Morgan's Colonial House, now **La Baie (The Bay)**, here after the floods of 1886 in the old city. Henry Birks, descendant of a long line of English jewellers, arrived soon after, establishing his famous shop in a handsome beige sandstone building on the west side of the square. In 1914, a monument to King Edward VII, sculpted by Philippe Hébert, was erected in the centre of Square Phillips.

A former Methodist church whose interior was designed as an auditorium, **St. James United Church** ★★ was built between 1887 and 1889 and originally had a complete facade looking out onto a garden. In 1926, in an

effort to counter a decrease in its revenues, the religious community built a stretch of stores and offices along the front of the building on Rue Sainte-Catherine, leaving only a narrow passageway into the church. However, the church recently underwent renovations that uncovered its impressive facade, complete with rose window, Gothic Revival towers and an elegant church yard.

After a 40-year absence, the Jesuits returned to Montréal in 1842 at Monseigneur Ignace Bourget's invitation. Six years later, they founded Collège Sainte-Marie, where several generations of boys

A winter scene in downtown Montréal.
© *Philippe Renault*

The interior of St. James United Church was laid out like an amphitheatre.
© *Québec Religious Heritage Foundation*

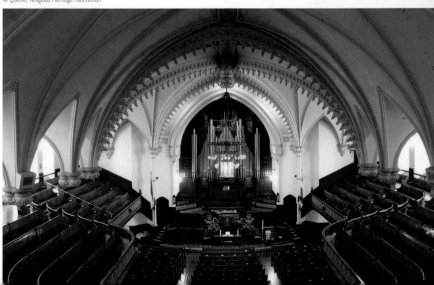

would receive an outstanding education. **Église du Gesù ★★** was originally designed as the college chapel. The grandiose project begun in 1864 was never completed, however, due to lack of funds. Consequently, the church's Renaissance Revival–style towers remain unfinished. The *trompe-l'œil* decor inside was executed by artist Damien Müller. Of particular interest are the seven main altars and surrounding parquetry, all fine examples of cabinet work. The large paintings hanging from the walls were commissioned from the Gagliardi brothers of Rome. The Jesuit college, erected to the south of the church, was demolished in 1975, but the church was fortunately saved and then restored in 1983.

Fleeing misery and potato blight, a large number of Irish immigrants came to Montréal between 1820 and 1860 and helped construct the Lachine Canal and the Victoria bridge. **St. Patrick's Basilica ★★** was built to meet a pressing new demand for a church to serve the Irish-Catholic community. When it was inaugurated in 1847, St. Patrick's dominated the city below. Today, it is well hidden by the skyscrapers of the business centre. Architect Pierre-Louis Morin and Père Félix Martin,

Club Soda, one of the many performance halls found in the Quartier des Spectacles.
© Martine Doyon – Quartier des spectacles

IT DON'T MEAN A THING IF IT AIN'T GOT THAT SWING: THE MONTREAL JAZZ FEST

From the small festival that was created in 1980 by Alain Simard, André Ménard and Denyse McCann on Île Sainte-Hélène, to today's major entertainment machine headed by Spectra, the recipe that has made this the world's largest jazz festival has remained the same: an eclectic program which features artists from all around the world, from local up-and-comers to the biggest names in jazz, and a wide selection of free outdoor concerts that attracts more than one million music lovers to the city's downtown core every summer.

the Jesuit superior, designed the plans for the edifice, built in the Gothic Revival style favoured by the Sulpicians, who financed the project. One of the many paradoxes surrounding St. Patrick's is that it is more representative of French than Anglo-Saxon Gothic architecture. The high, newly restored interior is spectacular in pale green, pink and gold. Each of the pine columns that divide the nave into three sections is a whole tree trunk, carved in one piece.

The heart of the **Quartier des Spectacles** *(www.quartierdesspectacles.com)* can be found at the intersection of Rue Sainte-Catherine and Boulevard Saint-Laurent. This one-square-kilometre entertainment district includes more than 30 performance halls with a total seating capacity of 28,000, art galleries and various venues for the exhibition and broadcast of alternative culture.

During the rush of the Quiet Revolution, the government of Québec, inspired by cultural complexes like New York's Lincoln Center, built **Place des Arts** ★, a grouping of five halls for the performing arts. The central Salle Wilfrid-Pelletier was inaugurated in 1963 (2,982 seats). It accommodates both the Montreal Symphony Orchestra and the Opéra de Montréal.

Place des Arts' Salle Wilfrid-Pelletier, home to the Montréal Symphony Orchestra. © Jean-Guy Bergeron

Downtown

The sculpture garden of the Musée d'Art Contemporain.

The cube-shaped building contains three theatres: Théâtre Maisonneuve (1,453 seats), Théâtre Jean-Duceppe (755 seats) and the intimate Studio-Théâtre (138 seats). The Cinquième Salle (350 seats) was built in 1992 during construction of the Musée d'Art Contemporain. Place des Arts is linked to the civil-service section of the underground city, which stretches from the Palais des Congrès convention centre to Avenue du Président-Kennedy. Developed by the various levels of government, this portion of the underground network distinguishes itself from the private section, centered around Place Ville Marie, farther west. The Place des Arts esplanade also serves as a cultural crossroads in the heart of the downtown sector. In summer, the stages of the city's major festivals are set up here.

The **Musée d'Art Contemporain de Montréal ★ ★**, Montréal's museum of modern art, was moved to this site in 1992. Both its size and the sheer volume of its collection, which includes more than 7,000 works, make it the largest contemporary-art museum in Canada. The long, low building, erected on top of the Place des Arts parking lot, contains five rooms where post-1940 works of art from both Québec and abroad are exhibited. The interior, which has a decidedly more attractive design than the exterior, is laid out around a circular hall. The museum's permanent exhibit features the

Since 1976, the head office of the Fédération des Caisses Populaires Desjardins, the credit union, has been located in the vast **Complexe Desjardins** ★, which also houses a large number of government offices. The building's large atrium surrounded by shops is very popular during the winter months. Various shows are presented in this space, which is surrounded by boutiques and a food court.

Erected in 1893 for the Société Saint-Jean-Baptiste, which is devoted to protecting the rights of French-speakers, the **Monument-National** ★ was intended to be a cultural centre dedicated to the French-Canadian cause, with its business courses, its platform for political orators and its presentation of various shows of a religious nature. However, during the 1940s, it also hosted cabaret shows and plays, launching the career of many a Québec performer, including Olivier Guimond Sr. and Jr. The building was sold to the National Theatre School of Canada in 1971. As Canada's oldest theatre, it was artfully restored for its 100th anniversary.

Montréal's **Chinatown** ★ may be small, but it is nonetheless a lovely place to explore. A large

largest collection of works by Paul-Émile Borduas, while its temporary exhibits usually favour multimedia creations. Among the museum's other facilities are the Olivieri bookshop, which specializes in monographs on Canadian artists and essays on art, and the La Rotonde restaurant, located above the Place des Arts esplanade. On the lower level, an amusing metal sculpture by Pierre Granche entitled *Comme si le temps... de la Rue* ("As if time... from the street") shows Montréal's network of streets crowded with helmeted birds in a sort of semicircular theatre.

The Musée d'Art Contemporain de Montréal's William Kentridge exhibit.
© Musée d'art contemporain de Montréal

The Palais des Congrès de Montréal's huge colourful facade as seen from indoors.

number of the Chinese who came to Canada to help build the transcontinental railroad, completed in 1886, settled here at the end of the 19th century. Though they no longer live in the neighbourhood, they still come here on weekends to stroll about and stock up on traditional products. Rue De La Gauchetière has been converted into a pedestrian street lined with restaurants and framed by beautiful Chinese-style gates.

The **Quartier International de Montréal (QIM)** ★★ business sector is the result of a major overhaul of the area located between Saint-Urbain, Saint-Jacques, University and Viger streets. The project, which was overseen by architect and urban planner Clément Demers with urban planner Réal Lestage,

won several prizes, including the prestigious *PMI Project of the Year*, awarded by the Project Management Institute in 2005. The area was long marred by the Ville-Marie expressway and neglected by Montrealers, but the QIM has made it a window onto Montréal's international economic activities.

The project entailed a profound urban restructuring effort that included the renovation of existing structures such as the Palais des Congrès, the addition of pedestrian walkways and green spaces and the construction of ultramodern buildings to house new businesses and hotels, all with the mandate of attracting foreign investors and improving local residential spaces. A 40% increase in pedestrian surfaces in this tran-

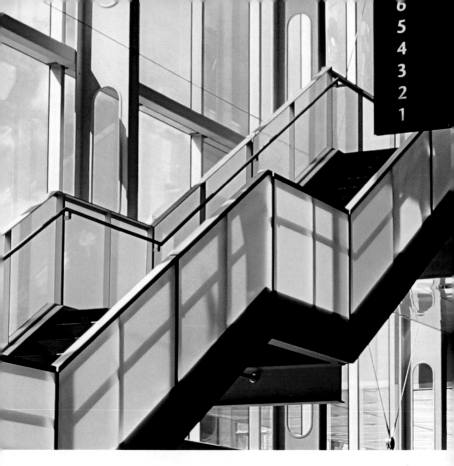

sitional area between downtown and Old Montréal was created by covering the Ville-Marie expressway between Rue Saint-Urbain and Square Victoria, adding public squares and widening the sidewalks. Furthermore, a series of poles bearing the flags of several of the world's countries now lines Rue University.

Montréal's convention centre, the **Palais des Congrès de Montréal ★**, partly built over the Ville-Marie expressway, used to contribute to the isolation of the old city from downtown. Work was completed in 2002 to double the size of the Palais des Congrès, which is now well integrated into the Quartier International.

Two works of art further enhance the Palais des Congrès: *Translucide*, a diptych by multimedia artists Michel Lemieux and Victor Pilon, among others, and *La Poussée Vers le Haut*, a mineral garden by Francine Larivée, on the roof. Two landscapes complete the decor: *Nature Légère / Lipstick Forest*, a surreal garden composed of 52 pink-concrete tree trunks, and *L'Esplanade*, where 31 heaps of dirt are linked by trails of Montréal-style limestone and planted with decorative crab-trees, the floral emblem of the City of Montréal since May 1995. Among the many works of public art that are found at the Palais des Congrès is also a sculpture by Charles Daudelin, *Éolienne V*, a stainless-steel mobile.

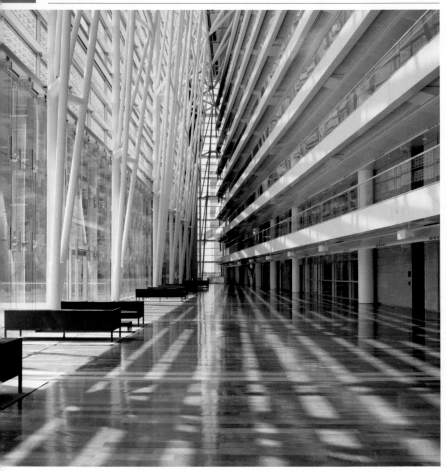

The magnificent gallery of the Centre CDP Capital, bathed in sunlight.
© Alain Laforest, photographer / Parquet-Centre CDP Capital

Downtown

A section of the Palais des Congrès now opens out onto street level. Its huge coloured-glass facade creates light effects both inside and outside the building. It overlooks the **Place Jean-Paul-Riopelle ★ ★** public square, at the corner of Saint-Antoine and De Bleury streets, where you will find an immense bronze sculpture-fountain created by Riopelle himself and entitled *La Joute*, complete with water jets and flames. In summer, mist blowers and underground lights add to the atmosphere and attract steady crowds. Across from the public square is the unique and imposing **Centre CDP Capital ★**, a business office of the Caisse de Dépôt et Placement du Québec (CDP).

During the 19th century, **Square Victoria** was a Victorian garden surrounded by Second Empire and Renaissance Revival stores and office buildings. Square Victoria was recently redesigned according to its original layout and is now one of the focal points of the Quartier International de Montréal. Square Victoria will eventually be given back its former shape and size, as well as its restored statue of Queen Victoria.

JEAN PAUL RIOPELLE

Jean Paul Riopelle was one of Québec's most renowned painters and its best-known internationally. Many of the impressive number of paintings he created are exhibited throughout the world. This legendary character, an abstract painter famous for his huge mosaics, left his mark on the world of contemporary art. He was born in Montréal in 1923, and his career took off with the Automatism movement in the 1940s. He was also one of the 16 co-signatories of the *Refus Global*, a cultural and political manifesto. He lived in Paris for several years, but returned to the province of Québec during the last years of his life. He died on March 12, 2002, in his manor on Île aux Grues, on the St. Lawrence River, in the migration path of the snow geese he held so dear to his heart.

Jean Paul Riopelle's *La Joute*, with water jets and a ring of fire.

An authentic Paris *métropolitain* gate stands at the entrance of the Square-Victoria metro station.
© Stéphan Poulin

Downtown

In 2003, the Quartier International de Montréal undertook the restoration of the "Entourage Grimard," named after architect Hector Grimard, who designed the Art-Nouveau gates to the Parisian "Métropolitain" in the early 1900s. The restoration was completed in collaboration with the Régie autonome des transports parisiens (RATP). During the ceremonies that surrounded the reopening of the "Entourage," which is set up at one of the exterior entrances to the Square-Victoria metro station, the RATP offered the previously loaned gate as a gift to the Société de Transport de Montréal (STM), making it the only authentic Grimard entrance outside Paris.

The headquarters of the two organizations that control international civil aviation, IATA (the International Air Transport Association) and ICAO (the International Civil Aviation Organization) are located in Montréal. The latter is a United Nations organization that was founded in 1947 and is located in the **Maison de l'OACI**, which houses the delegations of its 189 member countries. The back of the building, which has been connected to the Cité Internationale de Montréal, is visible from Square Victoria. *Miroir aux Alouettes*, a "stained-glass totem" by artist Marcelle Ferron, stands in front of the western facade of the building.

MONTRÉAL'S OUTDOOR MUSEUM

The City of Montréal's public art collection includes some 75 works that are integrated to the architecture of various buildings and another 225 that are set up in outdoor locations. Forming a veritable open-air museum, the works merge with their urban surroundings to become part of the daily scenery of Montrealers, who get to admire creative artistic endeavours for free.

The collection's diverse array of contemporary works, monuments, busts and sculptures reflects a great variety of artistic expressions, each piece embellishing a cultural centre, library, park, square or other public space in its own unique way.

The collection's oldest work is the Colonne Nelson (or Nelson Column), which was erected in 1809 on Place Jacques-Cartier, in Old Montréal. The column is also the first monument to have been built in memory of the Admiral—"The Hero of Trafalgar"—in all of the British Empire. Over the last few years, some 30 major works by artists from Québec and abroad have been added to the collection and Montréal's landscape.

Many Montréal citizens are first exposed to artistic expression through public art, and the presence of these works throughout the city should keep growing over the next few years. Indeed, an innovative program called *L'art public dans les arrondissements de Montréal* ("Public Art in the Boroughs of Montréal") was launched in October 2006, inviting the city's boroughs to develop public art projects that will further enhance the artistic character of Montréal and attract international visitors to this modern cultural metropolis.

La foule illuminée, by sculptor Raymond Mason, stands on Rue McGill College.

Montréal's World Trade Centre, a bridge between the past and the present.
© *World Trade Centre Montréal*

Downtown

World trade centres are exchange organizations intended to promote international trade. Montréal's **Centre de Commerce Mondial / World Trade Centre** ★ lies hidden behind an entire block of old facades. An impressive glassed-in passageway stretches over 180m through the centre of the building, along a portion of the Ruelle des Fortifications, a lane marking the former location of the northern wall of the fortified city.

Alongside the passageway, visitors will find a fountain and an elegant stone stairway, which provide the setting for a statue of Amphitirite, Poseidon's wife, taken from the municipal fountain in Saint-Mihiel-de-la-Meuse, France. This work of art dates back to the mid-18th century; it was created by Barthélémy Guibal, a sculptor from Nîmes, France, who also designed the fountains gracing Place Stanislas in Nancy, France. Visitors will also find a portion of the Berlin Wall, a gift from the City of Berlin on the occasion of the 350th anniversary of Montréal's foundation.

The skyline opens up at the end of Avenue McGill College, revealing a stunning view of Mount Royal and its cross.
© *Stéphan Poulin*

A spectacular sunset over the city skyline.
© Carlos Sanchez/Dreamstime.com

The Golden Square Mile

The Golden Square Mile, with its shady streets lined with sumptuous Victorian houses, was the residential neighbourhood of the Canadian upper class between 1850 and 1930. At its apogee, around the turn of the 20th century, an estimated 70% of the country's wealth lay in the hands of the area's residents, the majority of whom were of Scottish descent. Only a few houses from this era remain.

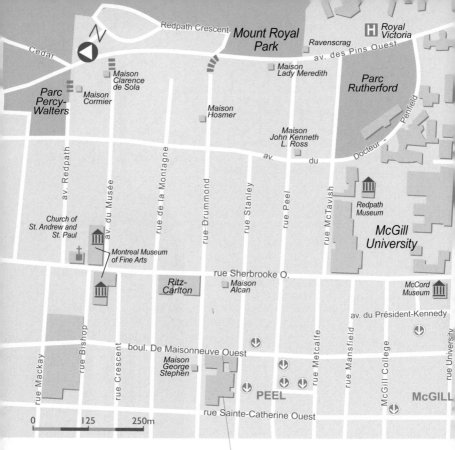

The **Montreal Museum of Fine Arts** ★ ★ ★ is the oldest and largest museum in Québec. It houses a variety of collections that illustrate the evolution of the fine arts from antiquity to the present day. The museum occupies three separate pavilions: the Michal and Renata Hornstein Pavilion, the Liliane and David M. Stewart Pavilion and the Jean-Noël Desmarais Pavilion. Only 10% of the museum's collection, which contains over 25,000 pieces in all, is on display. Furthermore, as many as three world-class temporary exhibitions can be presented at the museum simultaneously, which accounts for a significant portion of the institution's activity.

Known until 1948 as the Art Association of Montreal, the museum was founded in 1860, when the city was at the height of its glory, by a group of affluent art-loving Montrealers of British origin. The core of the permanent collection still reflects the taste of these wealthy families of English and Scottish descent, who donated many works to the museum. It wasn't until nearly 20 years later, however, that the museum was set up in its first exhibition space. With funds donated by local patron of the arts Benaiah Gibb, a modest art gallery, which no longer exists, was built near Square Phillips in 1879.

A subscription campaign was launched in 1909 to finance the construction of a more prestigious home for the museum, which would be erected in the heart of the former upper-class residential neighbourhood of Golden Square

The Michal and Renata Hornstein Pavilion of the Montreal Museum of Fine Arts.
© Christine Guest, MMFA

The Montreal Museum of Fine Arts' Canadian Art gallery.
© Brian Merrett, MMFA

Mile. This building, the present-day Michal and Renata Hornstein Pavilion, was inaugurated in 1912. Its architects graced it with an elegant, white Vermont-marble facade in the Classical Revival style, with lines reminiscent of ancient Rome. Expanded twice towards the back, in 1939 and in 1975, the building nonetheless ultimately proved to be too small.

Since demolishing the neighbouring buildings was out of the question, the museum's directors turned their attention to the property across the street, proposing an original solution and offering quite a challenge to their architect, Moshe Safdie, already well known for designing Habitat 67 and the National Gallery in Ottawa. The wing, named after Jean-Noël Desmarais, the father of arts patron Paul Desmarais, was inaugurated in 1991. On the left, it has a white marble facade, while incorporated into its right side is the red-brick facade of a former apartment building (1905). A series of underground passageways running beneath Rue Sherbrooke makes it possible to walk from the Jean-Noël Desmarais Pavilion to the Michal and Renata Hornstein Pavilion without ever stepping outside.

The Golden Square Mile

The Jean-Noël Desmarais Pavilion.
© Christine Guest, MMFA

Part of the decorative-arts collection at the Montreal Museum of Fine Arts.
© Christine Guest, MMFA

("Urban totem/History in lace"). For anyone interested in the First Nations and daily life in Canada in the 18th and 19th centuries, this is *the* museum to visit in Montréal. It houses a large ethnographic collection, as well as collections of costumes, decorative arts, paintings, prints and photographs, including the famous Notman photography collection, composed of 450,000 photos, including 200,000 glass negatives and constituting a veritable portrait of Canada at the end of the 19th century.

The **Musée McCord d'Histoire Canadienne / McCord Museum of Canadian History ★★** occupies a building formerly used by the McGill University Students' Association. Designed by architect Percy Nobbs (1906), this handsome building of English baroque inspiration was enlarged toward the back in 1991. Near Rue Victoria is an interesting sculpture by Pierre Granche entitled *Totem Urbain/Histoire en Dentelle*

McGill University ★★ was founded in 1821, thanks to a donation by fur-trader James McGill. It is the oldest of Montréal's four universities. Throughout the 19th century, the institution was one of the finest jewels of the Golden Square Mile's Scottish bourgeoisie. The university's main campus lies nestled in greenery at the foot of Mount

Detail of a magnificent totem at the McCord Museum.
© Productions Train d'enfer / SMQ

Royal. The focal point of the campus and the university's main entrance is the Roddick Gate, which contains the university's clock and chimes. Nearby are two Romanesque Revival buildings designed by Sir Andrew Taylor to house the physics (1893) and chemistry (1896) departments. The Faculty of Architecture now occupies the second building. A little farther along, visitors will see the Macdonald Engineering Building, a fine example of the English baroque-revival style, with a broken pediment adorning its rusticated portal (1908). At the end of the drive stands the oldest building on campus, the **Arts Building** (1839). For three decades, this austere neoclassical structure by architect John Ostell was McGill University's only building. It houses Moyse Hall, a lovely theatre dating back to 1926.

The profile of the unusual **Redpath Museum ★** stands out next to the Arts Building. It is a protorationalist openwork building concealed behind a composite facade. Precious objects relating to archaeology, botany, geology and palaeontology, accumulated by the university's researchers and

The McCord Museum of Canadian History occupies a handsome English Baroque-inspired building.
© McCord Museum of Canadian History

The Redpath Museum occupies the first Québec building that was specifically designed to accommodate a museum. © Courtesy of H.J. Hofmann, Redpath Museum

professors, have been collected here. This was the first building in Québec designed specifically as a museum, and it is also a rare example of a building with an iron and stone framework not intended for industrial or commercial purposes.

Near the museum are the university's library and Redpath Hall, equipped with a French-style mechanical organ. Baroque music concerts are often held in this lovely hall dominated by its visible wooden frame. The gargoyles and lavishly sculpted columns of the library are among the most sophisticated examples of the Romanesque Revival style in Canada.

James Ross House ★ was built in 1890 for the head engineer of Canadian Pacific. It now houses McGill University's Chancellor Day Hall. Expanded on several occasions, it was once the scene of glittering receptions. Its medieval castle-like appearance contributes to the charm of the Golden Square Mile. Particularly noteworthy is the combination of colours of its exterior, made up of a mixture of buff-coloured sandstone, pink granite and red slate. Since 1948, Chancellor Day Hall has been home to the McGill University Faculty of Law. A considerable portion of its large

The Arts Building, the oldest edifice on McGill University's campus. © McGill University

Palaeontology is one of the main themes at the Redpath Museum.

garden was lost when Avenue Docteur-Penfield was laid out in 1957.

Maison John Kenneth L. Ross ★ was originally the residence of James Ross' son, who lived in grand style for several years, accumulating yachts and race horses and travelling extensively. Once his father's fortune was exhausted, however, he had to sell the precious family collection of paintings at Christie's in London, a useless sacrifice in the end since the crash of 1929 ruined him anyway. His house (1909), a fine example of the Beaux-Arts style, is now an annex of the McGill University Faculty of Law.

Maison Lady Meredith ★ is perhaps Montréal's best example of the trend toward eclecticism, polychromy and the picturesque that swept through North America in the last two decades of the 19th century. Visitors will discover on its facades a mixture of styles ranging from Romanesque to late 18th century, as well as strong hues and a marvellous jumble of towers, inlays, bay windows and chimneys.

The Golden Square Mile

The Renaissance Revival-style Ravenscrag building dominates the city.
© McGill University

Maison Lady Meredith, with its elegant towers and chimneys.
© McGill University

During the 19th century, Montréal was not a political capital; it was first and foremost a commercial city endowed with an important port. Its castle was not that of a king, but rather that of a financial and commercial magnate. **Ravenscrag ★ ★** could indeed be labelled the castle of Montréal thanks to its prominent location overlooking the city, its exceptional size (originally over 60 rooms) and its history, which is rich in memorable receptions and prestigious hosts. This immense residence was built from 1861 to 1864 for the fabulously wealthy Sir Hugh Allan, who at the time had a near monopoly on sea transportation between Europe and Canada. From the central tower of his house, this "monarch" could keep a close eye on the comings and goings of his ships at the port.

Sir Hugh Allan's house is one of the best North-American examples of the Renaissance Revival style, inspired by Tuscan villas and characterized, notably, by an irregular plan and an observation tower. The interior, almost entirely destroyed when the building was converted into a psychiatric institute (1943), used to include a Second Empire–style ballroom that was able to accommodate 200 polka dancers. Interesting aspects around the building include a cast-iron entry gate, a gate house and luxurious stables that are now used as offices.

Maison Hosmer ★ is without question the most exuberant Beaux-Arts–style house in Montréal. Thick mouldings, twin columns and cartouches, all carved in red sandstone imported from Scotland, were sure to impress both visitors and business rivals. Edward Maxwell drew up the plans while his brother William was studying at the École des Beaux-Arts in Paris. The sketches sent from across the Atlantic clearly had a great influence on the design of this house, erected in 1900 for Charles Hosmer, who had ties with Canadian Pacific and 26 other Canadian companies. Each room was designed in a different style in order to serve as a showcase for the Hosmer family's diverse collection of antiques. The family lived here until 1969, at which time the house became part of McGill University's Faculty of Medicine.

The **Maison Clarence de Sola** ★ is an extremely exotic Hispano-Moorish-style residence that clearly stands out against the urban landscape of Montréal. The contrast is even more amusing the day after a snowstorm. The house was erected in 1913 for Clarence de Sola, the son of a rabbi of Portuguese descent.

The **Maison Cormier** ★★ was designed in 1930 for personal use by Ernest Cormier, architect of the Université de Montréal and the Supreme Court in Ottawa. He experimented with the house, giving each side a different look—Art Deco for the facade, monumental for the east side and distinctly modern for the back. The interior was planned in minute detail. Cormier created most of the furniture, while the remaining pieces were acquired at the 1925 Exposition des Arts Décoratifs in Paris. Though its Art Deco facade appears quite small, thanks to the steep incline of the terrain the house actually has four above-ground floors on its rear side. The entire building, now listed as a historic monument, has been carefully restored.

The Hispano-Moorish-style Maison Clarence de Sola.
© Philippe Renault

Maison Cormier and its Art Deco facade.
© Philippe Renault

Maison George Stephen, a veritable monument to the city's Scottish bourgeoisie.
© Mount Stephen Club

The sumptuous dining room of Maison George Stephen.
© Mount Stephen Club

The Golden Square Mile

The lovely presbyterian **Church of St. Andrew and St. Paul** ★★ was one of the most important institutions of the Scottish elite in Montréal. Built in 1932 as the community's third place of worship, it illustrates the endurance of the medieval style in religious architecture. The stone interior is graced with magnificent commemorative stained-glass windows. Those along the aisles came from the second church and are for the most part significant British pieces, such as the windows of Andrew Allan and his wife, produced by the workshop of William Morris after sketches by the famous English Pre-Raphaelite painter Edward Burne-Jones. The Scottish-Canadian Black Watch Regiment has been affiliated with the church ever since it was created in 1862.

The last of Montréal's old hotels, the **Ritz-Carlton** ★ was inaugurated in 1911 by César Ritz himself. For many years, it was the favourite gathering place of the Montréal bourgeoisie. Some people even stayed here year-round, living a life of luxury among the drawing rooms, garden and ballroom. Many celebrities have stayed at this sophisticated luxury hotel over the years, including Richard Burton and Elizabeth Taylor, who were married here in 1964.

Maison Alcan ★, the head office of the Alcan aluminum company, is a fine example of historical preservation and inventive urban restructuring. Five buildings along Rue Sherbrooke, including the lovely **Maison Atholstan**, the first Beaux-Arts–style structure erected in Montréal (1894), have been carefully restored and joined in the back to an atrium, which is linked to a modern aluminum building.

Lord Mount Stephen, born in Stephen Croft, Scotland, was a determined man. Co-founder and first president of Canadian Pacific, he built a transcontinental railroad stretching over 5,000km from New Brunswick to British Columbia. His house, **Maison George Stephen** ★★ is a veritable monument

Charming store fronts on Rue Crescent.

to Montréal's Scottish bourgeoisie. The house was built between 1880 and 1883 at a cost of $600,000, an astronomical sum at the time. Stephen called upon the best artisans in the world who covered the interior walls with marble, onyx and woodwork made of rare materials, such as English walnut, Cuban mahogany and Sri Lankan satinwood. The ceilings are so high that the house seems to have been built for giants. Since 1925, it has been owned by the Mount Stephen Club, a private club for business people.

Rue Crescent ★ has a split personality. Its northern portion is lined with old row houses which now accommodate antique shops and luxury boutiques, while its southern portion is crowded with night clubs, restaurants and bars, most with sunny terraces lining the sidewalks. For many years, Rue Crescent was known as the English counterpart of Rue Saint-Denis. Though it is still a favourite among American visitors, its clientele is more diversified now.

Bustling both day and night, Boulevard Saint-Laurent is commonly referred to as *The Main*. © www.boulevardsaintlaurent.com

The Milton-Parc District and "The Main"

The magnificent Milton-Parc District was previously known as the McGill Ghetto because of its proximity to the eponymous university. The area boasts a few unique architectural jewels and is a pleasant place to discover.

In 1860, the *religieuses hospitalières* (nursing nuns) of Saint-Joseph left the Hôtel-Dieu hospital founded by Jeanne Mance in 1643 in Old Montréal and moved to the foot of Mount Royal. In the following years, the nuns gradually sold off the remaining property in lots, laying out streets that were soon to be lined with early 20th century row houses. During the 1970s, Milton-Parc residents opposed a plan that threatened to destroy their neighbourhood: a number of the area's row houses were to be replaced by a massive real-estate development project. Only the first stage of this project ended up being built: the Complexe La Cité.

Between 1979 and 1982, the neighbourhood's residents managed to renovate their early-20th-century row houses by creating North America's largest housing cooperative with the support of Héritage Montréal, the Canadian Centre for Architecture's founder and director, Phyllis Lambert, and the financial backing of the Canada Mortgage and Housing Corporation.

The **Montreal Diocesan Theological College ★** is dedicated to the training of Anglican priests. With its densely ornamented walls of beige sandstone and red brick, the 1896 Gothic Revival–style building is representative of the picturesque, polychrome period of the end of the Victorian era.

Montréal's first hospital, the **Hôtel-Dieu ★** was founded in 1642 by Jeanne Mance and remains one of the city's major medical institutions. The institution and the city were founded almost simultaneously as part of a project initiated by a group of devout Parisians led by Jérôme Le Royer de La Dauversière. Thanks to the wealth of Angélique Faure de Bullion, wife of the superintendent of finances under Louis XIV, and the devotion of Jeanne Mance, the institution grew rapidly on Rue Saint-Paul in Old Montréal. However, lack of space, polluted air and noise in the old city forced the nuns to move the hospital to their farm in Mont-Sainte-Famille in the mid-19th century. The complex was expanded many times and is centered around a lovely neoclassical chapel with a dome and a facade reminiscent of urban churches in Québec under the French Regime. The interior, redesigned in 1967, has, however, been divested of several interesting paintings.

The **Musée des Hospitalières** ★ moved into the former chaplain's house, next door to the hospital chapel. It provides a detailed account of both the history of the Filles Hospitalières de Saint-Joseph, a community founded at the Hôtel-Dieu de La Flèche (Anjou, France) in 1634, and the evolution of medicine over the last three centuries. Visitors can see the former wooden stairway of the Hôtel-Dieu de La Flèche (1634), given to the City of Montréal by the French region of Sarthe in 1963. The piece was skilfully restored by the Compagnons du Devoir and incorporated into the museum's beautiful entrance hall.

Boulevard Saint-Laurent ★★ is also known as "The Main" because of its 18th-century status as the Faubourg Saint-Laurent's main artery leading inland from the river. It remains one of the city's most interesting cultural and commercial thoroughfares. First laid out within the city's fortifications in 1672 under the name "Saint-Lambert," "Rue Saint-Laurent" became Montréal's first and most important street to be extended northwards up to Rivière des Prairies. The street actually marks the boundary between eastern and

The Musée des Hospitalières neighbours the Hôtel-Dieu's chapel.

A streetcar travels along *The Main* in the 1940s.

Summer's festive Main Madness sidewalk sale.

© www.boulevardsaintlaurent.com

western Montréal, a demarcation that became official in 1792, when the street was known as "Saint-Laurent du Main" and often simply referred to as "The Main". In 1905, the city finally gave the street its current moniker, "Boulevard Saint-Laurent."

Around 1880, members of French-Canadian high society came up with the idea of turning the boulevard into the "Champ-Élysées" of Montréal. The west side was destroyed in order to make the street wider and to reconstruct new buildings in Richardson's Romanesque Revival style, which was all the rage at the end of the 19th century. Populated by successive waves of immigrants who arrived at the port, Boulevard Saint-Laurent never, however, attained the heights of glory anticipated by its developers. But the section between Boulevard René-Lévesque and Boulevard de Maisonneuve did become the hub of Montréal nightlife in the early 20th century. Indeed, the city's big theatres, like the Français, where Sarah Bernhardt performed, were located around here. During the Prohibition (1919-1930), the area became run-down. Every week, thousands of American vistors came here to frequent the cabarets and brothels, which abounded in this neighbourhood until the late 1950s.

Summer is a festive time on the Main. Boulevard Saint-Laurent band together twice every year to hold a huge sidewalk sale. One

The Milton-Parc District and "The Main"

DANIEL LANGLOIS AND EX-CENTRIS

Daniel Langlois, who founded Softimage in 1986, began his career in 1980 at the National Film Board's animation studios. With three colleagues, he created one of the first computer-animated short films, *Tony de Peltrie* (1985).

The 1995 sale of Softimage to Microsoft allowed him to make his dream come true: to build a centre for the production and distribution of films based on new technologies. Having hosted several major cultural events since its opening in 1999, Ex-Centris is now home to the Festival du Nouveau Cinéma, which was created in 1971.

Daniel Langlois is the recipient of many awards and honours. Having given himself the mission of promoting independent cinema and digital creation, he established a philanthropic foundation in his name in 1997.

The Milton-Parc District and "The Main"

of the city's busiest streets is then closed off to traffic between Rue Sherbrooke and Avenue du Mont-Royal, and pedestrians get to check out the bohemian crowd, shop for bargains and savour mangoes and piña coladas on outdoor terraces.

A cluster of family restaurants with terraces stretching all the way to the middle of the street can be found on **Rue Prince-Arthur**, a pedestrian street that was Montréal's bastion of hippie culture during the 1960s. On summer evenings, a dense crowd gathers between the buildings to applaud street performers.

Ex-Centris ★ is located in a stone building that blends well with the older buildings next to it. A film and new-media complex, Ex-Centris was opened in 1999 by Daniel Langlois, who financed the entire construction from beginning to end. The movie theatre screens the

The Ex-Centris film and new-media complex.
© Michel Legendre

best independent films, produced either locally or internationally, in three magnificent rooms of different sizes.

Montréal photographer William Notman, known for his Canadian scenes and portraits of 19th-century bourgeoisie, lived in the **Maison Notman** ★, on Rue Sherbrooke, from 1876 to 1891. The inexhaustible Notman photographic archives may be viewed at the

A horse-drawn sleigh in front of the Notman Studio on Rue De Bleury.
© I-10497 / McCord Museum, Montréal

McCord Museum of Canadian History. The house was erected in 1844 and is a fine example of the Greek Revival style as it was interpreted in Scotland in those years. Its extreme austerity is broken only by a few small, decorative touches, such as the palmettes and rosettes of the portico.

Set up inside the former Ekers brewery, the **Musée Juste Pour Rire / Just for Laughs Museum** ★ opened in 1993. This unique museum explores the different facets of humour using a variety of film clips and sets. The building itself also houses a concert hall, Le Cabaret Juste Pour Rire.

The Just for Laughs Museum.
© Just for Laughs Festival

Shaughnessy Village

When the Sulpicians took possession of the island of Montréal in 1663, they kept a portion of the best land for themselves, then set up a farm and a native village there in 1676. Following a fire, the native village was relocated several times before being permanently established in Oka. A part of the farm, corresponding to the area now known as Westmount, was then granted to French settlers. The Sulpicians planted an orchard and a vineyard on the remaining portion. Starting around 1870, the land was separated into lots. Part of it was used for the construction of mansions, while large plots were awarded to Catholic communities allied with the Sulpicians. It was at this time that Shaughnessy House was built—hence the name of the neighbourhood. During the 1970s, the number of local inhabitants increased considerably, making Shaughnessy Village the most densely populated area in Québec.

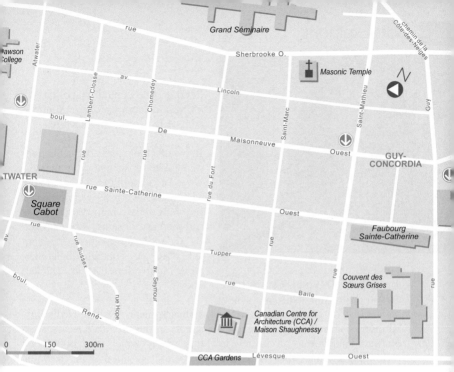

Masonic lodges, which had already existed in New France, increased in scale with British immigration. These associations of freethinkers were not favoured by the Canadian clergy, who denounced their liberal views. Ironically, the **Masonic Temple ★**, one of Montréal's Scottish lodges, stands opposite the Grand Séminaire, where Catholic priests are trained. The edifice, built in 1928, enhances the secret, mystical character of Freemasonry with its impenetrable, windowless facade, equipped with antique vessels and double-headed lamps.

It is well worth entering the **Grand Séminaire ★★** to see the lovely Romanesque Revival–style chapel designed by Jean Omer Marchand in 1905. The ceiling beams are made of cedar from British Columbia, while the walls are covered with stones from Caen. The 80m-wide nave is lined with 300 hand-carved oak pews. Sulpicians who have died in Montréal since the 18th century are interred beneath it.

The Masonic Temple, built in 1928.
© Québec Religious Heritage Foundation

The Sulpician order was founded in Paris by Jean-Jacques Olier in 1641, and its main church is the Saint-Sulpice in Paris, which stands on the square of the same name.

The Congrégation de Notre-Dame, founded by Marguerite Bourgeoys in 1671, owned a convent and a school in Old Montréal. Reconstructed in the 18th century, these buildings were expropriated by the city at the beginning of the 20th century as part of a plan to extend

Shaughnessy Village

The entrance to the Grand Séminaire.
© Abla Mansour

Revival–style central chapel has an elongated copper dome reminiscent of Byzantine architecture.

Between 1965 and 1975, Shaughnessy Village witnessed a massive wave of demolition. A great many Victorian row houses were replaced by residential high-rises, whose rudimentary designs, characterized by an endless repetition of identical glass or concrete balconies, were often referred to as "chicken coops."

Avenue Seymour ★ is one of the only streets in the area to have escaped this wave, which has now been curbed. It is lined with charming houses made of brick and grey stone, with Queen Anne, Second Empire or Romanesque Revival details.

Boulevard Saint-Laurent all the way to the port. The nuns had to leave the premises and settle into a new convent. The congregation thus arranged for a convent to be built on Rue Sherbrooke, according to a design by Jean Omer Marchand (1873-1936), the first French-Canadian architect to graduate from the École des Beaux-Arts in Paris. The immense complex, which is now home to the English-language **Dawson College** ★, bears witness to the vitality of religious communities in Québec before the Quiet Revolution of 1960. Its Romanesque

Founded in 1979 by Phyllis Lambert, the **Canadian Centre for Architecture** ★★★ is both a museum and a centre for the study of world architecture. Its collections of plans,

The Canadian Centre for Architecture Garden (Melvin Charney, artist).
© Canadian Centre for Architecture, Montréal / Photo Alain Laforest

PHYLLIS LAMBERT AND THE CCA

Since the late 1950s, Phyllis Lambert has contributed to several large-scale projects as a consulting architect or designer. But her major work, as consulting architect for designer Peter Rose, was the creation of the Canadian Centre for Architecture (CCA) in 1989, of which she was also the founder and first director.

This internationally renowned museum and study centre houses one of the world's largest collections of archival documents, books, photographs and architectural drawings. An expert in architectural preservation, Phyllis Lambert has published many works on such topics as the city of Montréal, and has received several awards and honorific doctorates. In 1997, her career was crowned by the prestigious Hadrian Award, bestowed by the World Monuments Fund (WMF).

drawings, models, books and photographs are the most important of their kind in the world.

The centre was erected between 1985 and 1989 and has six exhibition rooms, a bookstore, a library, a 217-seat auditorium and a wing specially designed for researchers, as well as vaults and restoration laboratories. The main building, shaped like a *U*, was designed by Peter Rose, with the help of Phyllis Lambert. It is covered with grey limestone from the Saint-Marc quarries near Québec City. This material, which used to be extracted from the Plateau Mont-Royal and Rosemont quarries in Montréal, also adorns the facades of many of the city's houses.

The Canadian Centre for Architecture, Montréal: view of the south elevation showing the Alcan Scholars' Wing (1989, Peter Rose, architect) and Shaughnessy House (1874, W.T. Thomas, architect), looking west.
© Canadian Centre for Architecture, Montréal - Photo Alain Laforest

Concordia University's Engineering, Computer Science and Visual Arts Complex.

© John Londoño

The centre surrounds the **Maison Shaughnessy** ★, whose facade looks out onto Boulevard René-Lévesque Ouest. This house is in fact a pair of residences, built in 1874. It is representative of the mansions that once lined Rue Dorchester.

In 1974, it was at the centre of an effort to salvage the neighbourhood, which had been torn down in a number of places. The house, itself threatened by demolition, was purchased at the last moment by Phyllis Lambert; she set up the offices and reception rooms of the Canadian Centre for Architecture inside. The building was named after Sir Thomas Shaughnessy, a former president of the Canadian Pacific Railway Company, who lived in the house for several decades. Neighbourhood residents who formed an association subsequently chose to name the entire area after him.

The amusing **Canadian Centre for Architecture Garden** ★, by artist Melvin Charney, lies across from Shaughnessy House between two highway on-ramps. It illustrates the different stages of the neighbourhood's development using a portion of the Sulpicians' orchard, stone lines to indicate borders of 19th-century properties and rose bushes reminiscent of the gardens of those houses. A promenade along the cliff that once separated the wealthy neighbourhood from the working-class sector below offers a view of the lower part of the

View of the Shaughnessy House Tea Room showing the I Feltri armchairs, the *La massa sciaccia le minoranze* table and the table with twelve legs designed by Gaetano Pesce.
© Canadian Centre for Architecture, Montréal - Photo Robert Burley / Design Archive 1990

The former **Couvent des Sœurs Grises ★**, which now belongs to Concordia University, is the product of an architectural tradition developed over the centuries in Québec. The chapel alone reveals a foreign influence, namely the Romanesque Revival style favoured by the Sulpicians, as opposed to the Renaissance and Baroque Revival styles preferred by the church. A crypt and the Chapelle de l'Invention-de-la-Sainte-Croix can be found in the centre of the convent, whose stained-glass windows come from the Maison Champigneulle in Bar-le-Duc, France.

Concordia University's Engineering, Computer Science and Visual Arts Complex is part of the "Quartier Concordia" (Concordia neighbourhood) project, which aims to modernise the university's rather timeworn infrastructures and meet the demands of its ever-growing student population. The ultramodern pavilion features a glass exterior and wood-panelled interior. Concordia University is Montréal's second English-language university.

city (Little Burgundy, Saint-Henri, Verdun) and the St. Lawrence River. Some of the highlights of this panorama are represented in a stylized manner, atop concrete posts.

Westmount and Southwestern Montréal

The wealthy residential city of Westmount is enclosed in the territory of the City of Montréal. Today home to more than 20,000 people, it has long been regarded as the bastion of the Anglo-Saxon elite in Québec. Its shady, winding roads on the southwestern side of the mountain are lined with Neo-Tudor and Neo-Georgian residences, most of which were built between 1910 and 1930.

© Québec en images

Detail of Westmount's City Hall.

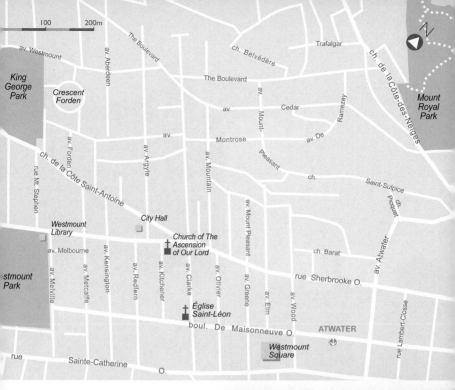

Architect Ludwig Mies van der Rohe (1886-1969), one of the leading masters of the modernist movement and the head of Bauhaus in Germany, designed **Westmount Square** ★★ in 1964. The complex is typical of the architect's North-American work, characterized by the use of black metal and tinted glass. It includes an underground shopping centre topped by three towers containing offices and apartments.

Several of Westmount's most fashionable shops can be found on **Avenue Greene** ★, a narrow street with a typically English-Canadian atmosphere. In addition to service-oriented businesses, there are art galleries, antique shops and bookstores filled with lovely coffee-table books.

Erected in 1928, Westmount's English Catholic church, the **Church of The Ascension of Our Lord** ★, bears

Westmount Square.
© *Québec en images*

Westmount's Neo-Tudor-style City Hall dominates the cityscape.

witness to the staying power of the Gothic-Revival style in North-American architecture and the historical accuracy, ever more apparent in the 20th century, of buildings patterned after ancient models. With its rough stone facing, elongated lines and detailed sculptures, it looks like an authentic church from a 14th-century English village.

Westmount is like a piece of Great Britain in North America. Its **City Hall ★** was built in the Neo-Tudor style, inspired by the architecture of the age of Henry VIII and Elizabeth I, which was regarded during the 1920s as the national style of England because it originated in the British Isles. The style is character-ized in part by horizontal openings with multiple stone transoms, bay windows and flattened arches.

In Québec, the term *côte*, which translates literally as "hill," usually has nothing to do with the slope of the land, but is rather a leftover division of the seigneurial system of New France. The roads linking one farm to the next ran along the tops of the long rectangles of land distributed to colonists. As a result, these plots of land gradually became known as *côtes*, from the French word for "side," *côté*. **Côte Saint-Antoine** is one of the oldest roads on the island of Montréal. Laid out in 1684 by the Sulpicians on a former Aboriginal trail, it is lined with some of Westmount's oldest houses. At the corner of Avenue Forden and Chemin de la Côte-Sainte-Catherine is a **milestone** dating back to the 17th century, discreetly identified by the pattern of the sidewalk, which radiates out from it. This is all that remains of the system of road signs developed by the Sulpicians for their seigneury on the island of Montréal.

King George Park offers the perfect combination of British and American atmospheres. The remains of a natural grouping of acacias, an extremely rare species at this latitude due to the harsh climate, can be found here.

Westmount Park ★ was laid out on swampy land in 1895. Four years later, Québec's first public library, the **Westmount Library**, was erected on the same site. Up until then, religious communities had been the only ones to develop this type of cultural facility, and the province was therefore somewhat behind in this area. The red-brick building is the product of the trends toward eclecticism, picturesqueness and polychromy that characterized the last two decades of the 19th century. A passageway leads to the **Westmount Conservatory**, whose greenhouses regularly present floral exhibits, and Victoria Hall, a former cultural centre that was built in 1924 in the same style as the city hall. Its art gallery shows works by local Westmount artists.

At the corner of Avenue Clarke stands the **Église Saint-Léon ★**, the only French-language Catholic parish in Westmount. The sober, elegant Romanesque Revival facade conceals an exceptionally rich interior decor begun in 1928 by artist Guido Nincheri.

The floor and the base of the walls are covered with the most beautiful Italian and French marble available, while the upper portion of the nave is made of Savonnières stone and the chancel of the most precious Honduran walnut, hand-carved by Alviero Marchi. The complex stained-glass windows depict various scenes from the life of Jesus Christ, as well as a few individ-

The Conservatory, a cultural institution in Westmount Park.
© Carlton Mceachern - FOTOLIA

The Parisian Laundry building hosts various exhibits.
© Parisian Laundry

uals from the time of the church's construction that visitors will be amused to discover among biblical figures.

Finally, the entire Christian pantheon is represented in the chancel and on the vault in vibrantly coloured frescoes, executed in the traditional manner of egg-wash. This technique (used, notably, by Michelangelo) consists of making pigment stick to a wet surface with a coating made of egg, which becomes very hard and resistant when dry.

In 1897, local reformist Herbert Browne Ames published *The City Below the Hill*, a work that stands out in the history of urban-renewal movements. It revealed the decrepit state of Montréal's working-class neighbourhoods at the end of the 19th century, and most notably that of Saint-Henri, or Saint-Henri-des-Tanneries, as this former city was known before it was annexed to Montréal in 1905. After the opening of the Lachine Canal in 1825, the little town grew significantly, with industries clustering in its southern portion around the canal.

However, the opening of the St. Lawrence Seaway in 1959 and the subsequent closing of the canal in 1970 led

to the decline of the neighbourhood. Westmount Hill, surrounded by luxurious residences and luscious gardens further highlighting the contrast between the upper and lower parts of the city, can be seen when looking north from many of Saint-Henri's streets.

A former commercial laundry facility, **Parisian Laundry** ★ is one of the neighbourhood's rehabilitated industrial buildings that are now used to promote cultural endeavours. Its concrete-and-steel structure and large windows provide the perfect setting for artistic exhibits.

Historically, the upper-class residents of Saint-Henri lived along Rue Saint-Antoine. Beautiful **Square Saint-Henri** ★, adorned with a cast-iron fountain topped with a copy of the statue of Jacques Cartier (1893) that can be found within the Place-Saint-Henri metro station, was a gathering point for the municipality's affluent residents.

Marché Atwater ★ is one of Montréal's large public markets. Its elegant Art Deco building was built in 1932 as part of the job-creation programs that were initiated during the Great Depression (1929).

On the other side of the Lachine Canal lies Pointe Saint-Charles, which was named by fur traders Charles Le-Moyne and Jacques LeBer, to whom the piece of land was first granted. They then sold it to Marguerite Bourgeoys, who built the Ferme Saint-Gabriel for the Sœurs de la Congrégation de Notre-Dame here in 1668.

Maison Saint-Gabriel ★★ offers precious evidence of what daily life was like in New France. The farmhouse and adjoining barn were built between 1662 and 1698. The house later served as a school for young Aboriginal girls and as accommodations for the "Filles du Roy" (Kings Daughter's), the young women that Louis XIV sent to Montréal to help populate France's colony. The house was restored and opened to the public in 1966.

Maison Saint-Gabriel bears witness to daily life in New France during the 17th century. © Pierre Guzzo, Maison Saint-Gabriel

© Patrick Escudero

Quartier Latin

The Quartier Latin, a university neighbourhood centered around Rue Saint-Denis, is popular for its theatres, cinemas and countless outdoor cafés, which offer a view of the area's heterogeneous crowd of students and revellers. The district's origins date back to 1823, when Montréal's first Catholic cathedral, Église Saint-Jacques, was established on Rue Saint-Denis. This prestigious edifice quickly attracted the cream of French-Canadian society to the area, mainly old noble families who had remained in Canada after the conquest. In 1852, a fire ravaged the neighbourhood, destroying the cathedral and Monseigneur Bourget's palace. Painfully reconstructed in the second half of the 19th century, the area remained residential until the Université de Montréal was established here in 1893, marking the beginning of a period of cultural turmoil that would eventually lead to the Quiet Revolution of the 1960s. The Université du Québec à Montréal (UQAM), founded in 1969, has since replaced the Université de Montréal, which is now located on the north side of Mount Royal. The presence of the university has ensured the Quartier Latin's prosperity

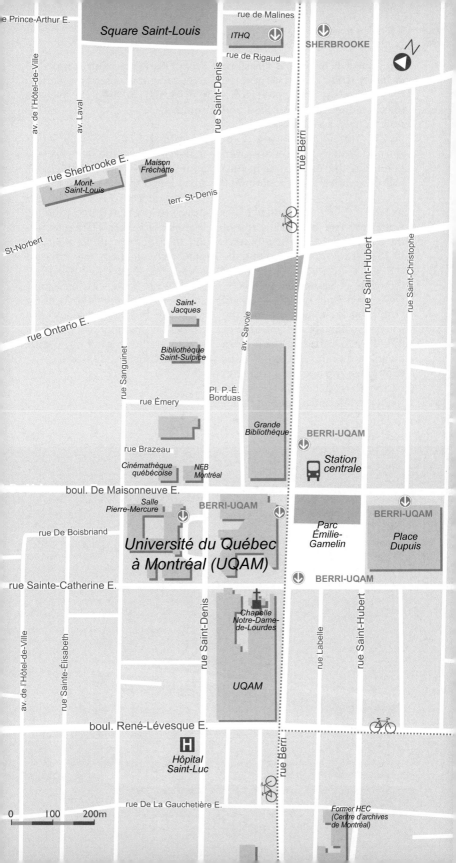

The **Institut de Tourisme et d'Hôtellerie du Québec (ITHQ)**, a school devoted to the tourism and hotel industries, was recently renovated and now features an ultramodern glass facade. Top-notch cooking, tourism and hostelry courses are given here, and the establishment also features a hotel and a restaurant.

In 1848, the City of Montréal had a water reservoir built at the top of the hill known as Côte-à-Barron. In 1879, it was dismantled and the site was converted into a park by the name of **Square Saint-Louis ★ ★**. Developers built beautiful Second Empire–style homes around the square, making it the nucleus of the French-Canadian bourgeois neighbourhood. These groups of houses give the area a certain harmonious quality that is rarely found in Montréal's urban landscape. **Rue Prince-Arthur** is a pedestrian street that extends west from the square and is quite lively in summer.

Avenue Laval is one of the only streets in the city where the Belle Époque atmosphere is still very evident. Abandoned by the French-Canadian bourgeoisie in 1920, its houses were first converted into rooming houses before they started attracting the attention of local artists, who restored them one by one. Poet Émile Nelligan (1879-1941) lived at no. 3688 with his family at the turn of the 20th century. A bronze bust by artist Roseline Granet in memory of the poet stands at the corner of Avenue Laval and Square Saint-Louis.

The ultramodern facade of the Institut de Tourisme et d'Hôtellerie du Québec.
© Pierre Beauchemin, Institut de Tourisme et d'Hôtellerie du Québec

Peaceful Square Saint-Louis in winter.

In 1992, the **Maison des Écrivains** opened in the former home of filmmaker Claude Jutra, who directed such films as *Mon Oncle Antoine*. A number of other artists, including singer Pauline Julien and her late husband, poet and politician Gérald Godin, filmmaker Gilles Carle and his spouse Chloé Sainte-Marie, writers Michel Tremblay and Yves Navarre, and pianist André Gagnon, live or have lived in the area around Square Saint-Louis and Avenue Laval.

Mont-Saint-Louis ★, a former boys' school run by the brothers of the Écoles Chrétiennes, was built facing straight up Avenue Laval in 1887. The long facade punctuated with pavilions, grey stone walls, openings with segmental arches and mansard roof, make this building one of the most characteristic examples of the Second Empire style as adapted to suit Montréal's big institutions. The school closed

its doors in 1970 and the edifice was converted into an apartment building in 1987, at which time an unobtrusive parking lot was built under the garden.

Journalist, poet and Member of Parliament Louis Fréchette (1839-1908) lived in the **Maison Fréchette** a Second Empire-style house. Sarah Bernhardt stayed here on several occasions during her North-American tours.

Montréal architect Joseph-Arthur Godin was one of the precursors of modern architecture in North America. In 1914, he began construction on three apartment buildings with visible reinforced concrete frames in the Quartier Latin area. One of these is the **Saint-Jacques** ★. Godin blended this avant-garde concept with subtle Art-Nouveau curves, giving the buildings a light, graceful appearance. The venture was a com-

Quartier Latin

A former boys' school, Mont-Saint-Louis was built in 1887.

© Jean-Louis Desrosiers

mercial failure, however, leading Godin to bankruptcy and ending his career as an architect.

The **Bibliothèque Saint-Sulpice** ★ was originally built for the Sulpicians, who looked unfavourably upon the construction of a public library on Rue Sherbrooke. Even though many works were still on the *Index*, therefore forbidden reading for the clergy, the new library was seen as unfair competition. The library was an annex

of the Bibliothèque Nationale du Québec until the opening of the Grande Bibliothèque. It was designed in the Beaux-Arts style in 1914. This style, a synthesis of classicism and French Renaissance architecture, was taught at the École des Beaux-Arts in Paris, hence its name in North America. The interior is graced with lovely stained-glass windows created by Henri Perdriau in 1915.

The offices of **NFB Montréal** are home to Montréal's distribution and consultation branch of the National Film Board of Canada (NFB). Its facilities include the Cinérobothèque, which provides users with 21 viewing units (individual or double) to watch various films and documentaries.

The **Cinémathèque Québécoise** ★ is another great place for movie lovers. It features a collection of 25,000 Canadian, Québécois and foreign films, as well as several pieces of equipment that date back to the early days of cinema. In addition, the Cinémathèque contains

The Cinémathèque Québécoise on Boulevard De Maisonneuve.   © Cinémathèque québécoise

The spacious interior of the Grande Bibliothèque.

theatres, exhibit spaces, a "media-thèque" and a shop, as well as a café-bar. Facing it is a concert hall affiliated to the Université du Québec à Montréal, the **Salle Pierre-Mercure** of the Centre Pierre-Péla-deau.

The **Grande Bibliothèque** ★★ opened on April 30, 2005. This major addi-tion to Montréal's cultural land-scape cost nearly 100 million dol-lars and is housed in a bright and airy luxurious six-storey build-ing. The edifice's design features contrasting wood and glass ele-ments, while the library contains over four million titles, making it the most important collection of books and multimedia documents in the province. Though some say the establishment's inaugura-tion marks the death of neighbour-hood libraries, others argue that it meets the modern needs of the major cultural metropolis that is Montréal, especially after UNESCO named it a "World Book Capital City" for the year 2005-2006.

Unlike most North-American uni-versities, whose buildings are contained within a specific cam-pus, the campus of the **Université du Québec à Montréal (UQAM)** ★ is integrated into the city fabric like

Quartier Latin

The Biological Sciences Pavilion at Université du Québec à Montréal.
© Photo UQAM

French and German universities built during the Renaissance. It is also linked to the underground city and the metro. The university is located on the site once occupied by the buildings of the Université de Montréal and the Église Saint-Jacques, which was reconstructed after the fire of 1852. Only the wall of the right transept and the Gothic Revival steeple were integrated into the Pavillon Judith-Jasmin (1979), and these elements have since become the symbol of the university. UQAM is part of the Université du Québec, founded in 1969 and established in cities across the province. Every year, over 40,000 students attend this flourishing institution of higher learning.

Artist Napoléon Bourassa lived in a large house on Saint-Denis Street (no. 1242); its facade bears a "tête à Papineau," a bust of the great 19th century political figure. Louis-Joseph Papineau. The **Chapelle Notre-Dame-de-Lourdes** ★, erected in 1876, was his greatest achievement. It was commissioned by the Sulpicians, who wanted to secure their presence in this part of the city. Its Roman-Byzantine style is in some way a summary of its author's travels. The little chapel's recently restored interior, adorned with Bourassa's vibrantly coloured frescoes, is a must-see.

Parc Émilie-Gamelin ★, laid out in 1992 for Montréal's 350th anniversary, is a large public space that honours the memory of the founder of the Soeurs de la Providence religious order, whose asylum occupied this site until 1960. At the north end of the park are a few unusual metal sculptures by Melvin Charney, who also designed the Canadian Centre for Architecture Garden.

Quartier Latin

Université du Québec à Montréal's Judith-Jasmin Pavilion.
© Photo UQAM

The Beaux-Arts-style former École des Hautes Études Commerciales.
© Archives - HEC Montréal

A symbol of the social ascent of a certain class of French-Canadian businessmen in the early 20th century, the former **École des Hautes Études Commerciales** ★ ★ business school profoundly altered Montréal's managerial and financial circles. Prior to the school's existence, these fields were dominated by Canadians of British extraction. This imposing building's Parisian Beaux-Arts architecture (1908), characterized by twin columns, balustrades, a monumental staircase and sculptures, bears witness to the Francophile leaning of those who built it. In 1970, this

business school, known as HEC, joined the campus of the Université de Montréal on the north side of Mount Royal. This beautiful building faces Square Viger and now houses the Centre d'Archives de Montréal.

Quartier Latin

The symbolic rainbow flag of Gay Pride.

© iStockphoto.com / Arpad Benedek

The Village

Discover the Village, whose friendly and lively denizens flock to their neighbourhood cafes, restaurants and bars at all times of the day and night.

This neighbourhood, located on the edge of the downtown area, was developed in the late 18th century when Old Montréal extended eastward. Originally known as "Faubourg Québec" because it ran alongside the road leading to Québec City, it was renamed "Quartier Sainte-Marie" after becoming industrialized, then nicknamed "Faubourg à M'lasse" around 1880, when hundreds of barrels of sweet-smelling molasses were unloaded every day onto the wharves of the nearby port (*mélasse* is French for molasses).

In the mid-1960s, civil servants affixed the somewhat bland name "Centre-Sud" to the neighbourhood. This was before the homosexual community took it over in 1980 and made it the "Gay Village." Despite its many names, The Village is a place with a lot of spirit, and, given a chance, can be quite fascinating.

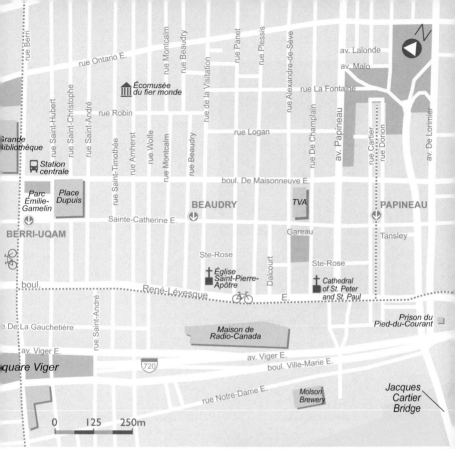

The map contains the following labels:

rue Berri, rue Ontario E., rue Montcalm, rue Beaudry, rue Panet, rue Plessis, av. Lalonde, av. Malo, rue La Fontaine, rue Alexandre-de-Sève, rue De Champlain, rue Papineau, rue Cartier, rue Dorion, av. De Lorimier, Écomusée du fier monde, rue Robin, rue Saint-Hubert, rue Saint-Christophe, rue Saint-André, rue Saint-Timothée, rue Amherst, rue Wolfe, rue Montcalm, rue de la Visitation, rue Logan, Grande Bibliothèque, Station centrale, boul. De Maisonneuve E., Parc Émilie-Gamelin, Place Dupuis, BEAUDRY, TVA, PAPINEAU, Sainte-Catherine E., Gareau, Tansley, BERRI-UQAM, Ste-Rose, Dalcourt, Ste-Rose, boul., René-Lévesque, Église Saint-Pierre-Apôtre, Cathedral of St. Peter and St. Paul, E., e. De La Gauchetière, rue Saint-André, Maison de Radio-Canada, Prison du Pied-du-Courant, av. Viger E., av. Viger E., boul. Ville-Marie E., square Viger, 720, rue Notre-Dame E., Molson Brewery, Jacques Cartier Bridge, 0 125 250m

Located in a former bathhouse, the Écomusée du Fier Monde is dedicated to the history of industry and labour.
© Julie Landreville, Écomusée du Fier Monde

The Village is divided into three zones of varying sizes from south to north: the port and industrial area along Autoroute Ville-Marie; the Maison de Radio-Canada, whose 1970 construction led to the demolition of a third of the neighbourhood; and, finally, Rue Sainte-Catherine and its large concentration of cafés, nightclubs, restaurants and bars can be found.

Those interested in the history of industry and labour and how the industrial revolution transformed this district can visit the **Écomusée du Fier Monde ★**. The museum is set up in a former bathhouse that was built in 1927 and modelled after the Butte-aux-Cailles pool in Paris. The social

The Maison de Radio-Canada tower.
© Jean Bernier

An oversized structure set like an island in the middle of a vast parking lot is visible from the end of the small Rue Beaudry. This is the **Maison de Radio-Canada**, which was built between 1970 and 1973. The building accommodates the province's French-language and local English-language programming of the CBC, or Canadian Broadcasting Corporation (Société Radio-Canada in French), the national radio and television network. When it was built, the traditional urban fabric of the neighbourhood was completely erased, as nearly 5,000 people (678 families) had to be relocated. Twenty years earlier, the city had also tripled the width of Boulevard René-Lévesque (formerly Dorchester Street) , separating the south part of the neighbourhood from the north.

and economic history of the neighbourhood is presented in a wonderfully rehabilitated interior.

Originally clustered in the "West" along Rue Stanley and Rue Drummond, gay bars were considered too conspicuous by some local real-estate developers and town councillors. The continual badgering and periodic attempts to "clean house" led bar owners, then renters in the downtown area, to purchase inexpensive buildings in the Centre-Sud in the hopes of running their businesses as they pleased. Thus was born the **Gay Village**, a concentration of establishments catering to a homosexual clientele (saunas, bars, restaurants, clothing stores and hotels). Far from being hidden or mysterious, many of these establishments open out onto the street with terraces and gardens during the warm summer months.

The **Église Saint-Pierre-Apôtre** ★ ★ is part of the monastery of the Oblate priests, who settled in Montréal in 1848 thanks to the assistance of Monseigneur Ignace Bourget. The building, completed in 1853, is a major work of Québec Gothic Revival architecture. Its notable features include flying buttresses, exterior supports for the walls of the nave that were rarely used in Montréal, and a spire, which measures 70m at its tallest point, an exceptional height for the time. The finely decorated interior reveals a number of other

Église Saint-Pierre-Apôtre and its limestone pillars.
© Québec Religious Heritage Foundation

Looking down on Rue Sainte-Catherine from the Jacques-Cartier Bridge.

uncommon elements, such as the limestone pillars separating the nave from the side aisles, here in a land where church structures were usually made entirely of wood. Some of the stained-glass windows from the Maison Champigneulle in Bar-le-Duc, France, deserve careful examination, most notably the choir's 9m-tall *Saint Peter* (1854).

The neoclassical presbytery of Saint-Pierre-Apôtre and the former buildings of the Maîtrise Saint-Pierre, a choir school and priests' residence, have been converted into a com-

The Village

GAY PRIDE

In Montréal, the Gay Pride Parade (or rather the LGBT—lesbian, gay, bisexual, transsexual and transvestite—Parade) is the starting point of the Festival Divers/Cité. A week of celebration that concludes with a great outdoor party, the festival is an opportunity to rejoice during which the homosexual community enjoys the luxury of taking to the streets to assert not only its acceptance, but its pride in being what it is.

A festive event that brings together all orientations and styles, the Festival Divers/Cité is characterized by a spirit of openness to the world. An event that combines an expression of difference with a demand for equality, it is one of the largest annual gatherings of homosexual communities in the world.

munity centre. **Rue Sainte-Rose** is a picturesque street, lined to the north with a series of working-class homes with mansard roofs. It has preserved part of its old-fashioned appearance. Since 1975, a number of neighbourhood houses have been restored by executives and artists working at nearby Radio-Canada.

The layout of **Rue Dalcourt**, a secondary street located between two main arteries, was patterned after London's mews. It is lined with

cramped housing that was originally intended for the area's poorest workers.

The offices of the **TVA** television network occupy an entire block. Founded in 1961 by Alexandre de Sève under the name Télé-Métropole, this private television network out-rated Radio-Canada among working-class viewers for many years. Some of the network's studios are located inside the former Théâtre Arcade and the Pharmacie Gauvin (1911), a handsome four-storey building

The Molson Brewery industrial complex overlooks the St. Lawrence River.
© Molson Brewery Canada

A portrait of John Molson, the brewery's founder.
© Molson Brewery Canada

The Beaudry metro station on Rue Sainte-Catherine, in the heart of the city's Gay Village. © Philippe Renault

made of glazed, white terra cotta. TVA, along with Radio-Canada and Télé-Québec, forms a veritable Cité des Ondes ("Broadcasting City") in south-central Montréal.

The **Cathedral of St. Peter and St. Paul** ★ is Montréal's Russian Orthodox Cathedral. The building, a former Episcopal church, was erected in 1853 and features a lovely collection of icons and treasures from Russia.

The **Molson Brewery** was opened back in 1786 in the Faubourg Qué-bec by an Englishman named John Molson (1763-1836). It would later become one of the most successful businesses in Canada. Its current facilities are visible from Boulevard René-Lévesque. The brewery's en-trance hall contains enlargements of photographs from the company ar-chives, as well as a souvenir shop.

Jacques Cartier Bridge ★ ★ was inaug-urated in 1930. Up until then, the Pont Victoria, completed in 1860, was the only means of reaching the

St. Lawrence River's south shore, aside from the ferry. The bridge also made it possible to link Île Sainte-Hélène directly to the central neigh-bourhoods of Montréal. It was a real nuisance to build because city coun-cillors couldn't agree on a plan that would avoid demolishing all sorts of buildings. It was finally decided that the bridge should be curved on its way into Montréal, earning it the nickname of "pont croche" (crooked bridge). Today, it is possible to cross the Jacques Cartier Bridge on foot (the sidewalk is on the bridge's east side), by bicycle (the bike path is on the west side) and of course by car, which is what thousands of motor-ists do every day to get to work.

Prison du Pied-du-Courant ★ ★ is named "Foot-of-the-Current" be-cause it is located in front of the river, at the foot of the Sainte-Marie current, which used to create resist-ance for ships entering the port. Built between 1830 and 1836, it is a long, neoclassical cut-stone building with a gate made of the same ma-

The Village

The former Pied-du-Courant prison and its handsome Monument to the Patriotes.
© MNP

The Jacques-Cartier Bridge dominates the Village.
© Alain Juteau / Dreamstime.com

terial. It is the oldest public building still standing in Montréal.

In 1894, a house for the prison warden was added at the corner of Avenue De Lorimier. In 1912, the last prisoners left Pied-du-Courant, which became the head office of the Commission des Liqueurs, the liquor commission, in 1922. Over the years, annexes and warehouses were added to the old forgotten prison. Between 1986 and 1990, however, the Québec government proceeded to demolish the additions and restore the prison, rekindling old memories of tragic events that took place shortly after it was opened.

It was within these walls that 12 of the Patriotes who participated in the armed rebellion of 1837-38 were executed. One of them was the Chevalier de Lorimier, after whom the neighbouring street was named. Five hundred others were imprisoned here before they were deported to the penal colonies of Australia and Tasmania in the South Pacific. A handsome **Monument to the Patriotes** ★ by Alfred Laliberté stands on the grounds of the former prison. The Gothic Revival warden's residence now houses the reception rooms of the Societé des Alcools du Québec (SAQ).

Located in the basement of the Édifice du Pied-du-Courant is the **Centre d'Exposition de la Prison-des-Patriotes**, an SAQ project that is run by the Maison Nationale des Patriotes and the Musée de Saint-Eustache et de ses Patriotes. Here, you can enjoy a theme exhibit on the 1837 and 1838 rebellion, which features seven sections: Introduction, Economy, Identity, Politics, Before Arms, To Arms! and Conclusion.

Hochelaga-Maisonneuve

In 1883, the city of Maisonneuve was founded in eastern Montréal by farmers and French-Canadian merchants; port facilities then expanded into the area in 1889 and the city's development picked up. In 1918, the formerly autonomous city was annexed to Montréal, becoming one of its major working-class neighbourhoods, with a 90% francophone population. In the course of its history, Maisonneuve has been profoundly influenced by men with grand ideas who wanted to make this part of the province a place where people could thrive together. Upon taking office at the Maisonneuve town hall in 1910, brothers Marius and Oscar Dufresne instituted a rather ambitious policy of building prestigious Beaux-Arts–style public buildings intended to make "their" city a model of development for French Québec. Then, in 1931, Brother Marie-Victorin founded Montréal's botanical garden in Maisonneuve, which remains one of the largest in the world. The last major episode in the area's history took place in 1971, when Mayor Jean Drapeau initiated construction of the immense sports complex that was used for the 1976 Olympic Games.

© Biodôme de Montréal

Penguin, Biodôme de Montréal.

Construction of the **Montréal Botanical Garden** ★★★, or the Jardin Botanique de Montréal as it is known in French, was first undertaken during the economic crisis of the 1930s on the site of Mont-de-La-Salle, home base of the brothers of the Écoles Chrétiennes, by Brother Marie-Victorin, a well-known Québécois botanist. Behind the Art Deco-style building occupied by the botanical garden's administrative offices is a stretch of 10 connected greenhouses. Open year-round, these greenhouses shelter a precious collection of orchids and a part of the largest grouping of bonsais and *penjings* outside Asia. The latter includes the famous Wu collection, given to the garden by master Wu Yee-Sun of Hong Kong in 1984. The cucurbitaceae family of vegetables takes the spotlight in the main greenhouse in October: over 600 pumpkins are decorated to celebrate Halloween, much to the delight of the many young visitors who drop by for this event.

Hochelaga-Maisonneuve

THE BOTANICAL GARDEN

Founded in 1931 by Brother Marie-Victorin, the Montréal Botanical Garden is one of the world's largest and today welcomes nearly one million visitors each year. A major international attraction in Montréal, it features some 22,000 plant species and cultivars from every corner of the globe. Its exhibition greenhouses house 6,000 species and cultivars, including several rare and endangered plants. Exterior gardens include the Alpine Garden, the Shade Garden and the Perennial Garden, while cultural diversity in the botanical world is reflected in the First-Nations Garden, the Chinese Garden and the Japanese Garden.

Red berries covered in frost in the winter garden.
© Gilles Murray, Montréal Botanical Garden

Orchid.
© Gilles Murray, Montréal Botanical Garden

Thirty outdoor gardens, open from spring to autumn and designed to educate and amaze visitors, stretch to the north and west of the greenhouses. Particularly noteworthy are a beautiful rosary, the Japanese garden and its *sukiya*-style pavilion, as well as the very lovely Lac de Rêve's Jardin de Chine garden, whose pavilions were designed by artisans who came here from China specific-

Ladybug.
© Gilles Murray, Montréal Botanical Garden

Gold lion tamarin, Biodôme de Montréal.
© Sean O'Neil

ally for the task. Since Montréal is the twin city of Shanghai, it was deemed appropriate that it should have the largest such garden outside Asia. During late-summer nights, the Chinese Garden is decorated with hundreds of Chinese lanterns that create a wonderful fairytale-like setting of light and flowers.

Another must-see is the First Nations Garden. Inaugurated in 2001, it is the result of efforts by several contributors, both Aboriginal and non-Aboriginal, including Brother Marie-Victorin, who was hoping to integrate a garden of medicinal plants used by Aboriginal communities. His achievement allows the uninitiated to familiarize themselves with the Aboriginal world, especially their use of plants. Québec's 11 First Nations are represented in their natural habitat areas: deciduous forests, mixed-wood forests and the Nordic zone. An exhibition pavilion completes the tour.

The northern part of the botanical garden is occupied by an arboretum. The **Maison de l'Arbre**, or "tree house," was established in this area to educate people about the life of trees. The interactive, permanent exhibit is actually set up in an old tree trunk. There are displays on the yellow birch, Québec's emblematic tree, while the building's structure, consisting of different types of wood beams, reminds us how leafy forests really are. The play of light and shade from the frame onto the large white wall, meant to resemble trunks and branches, is particularly noteworthy. The terrace in the back is an ideal spot from which to contemplate the

The Château Dufresne, styled after Versailles' Petit Trianon.   © *Michel Gingras, Musée du Château Dufresne*

arboretum's pond; it also leads to a charming little North-American bonsai garden.

The **Montréal Insectarium** ★ is located east of the greenhouses. This innovative, living museum invites visitors to discover the fascinating world of insects through interactive games and an impressive collection of specimens.

Château Dufresne ★ ★ is in fact two 22-room private mansions behind the same facade, built in 1916 for brothers Marius and Oscar Dufresne, shoe manufacturers and authors of a grandiose plan to develop Maisonneuve. The plan was abandoned after the onset of World War I, causing the municipality to go bankrupt. Their home, designed by Marius Dufresne and Parisian architect Jules Renard, was supposed to be the nucleus of a residential upper-class neighbourhood, which never materialized. It is one of the best examples of Beaux-Arts architecture in Montréal. Château Dufresne now houses temporary exhibitions, as well as a collection of furniture.

The **Olympic Stadium** ★ ★ ★, known in French as the Stade Olympique, is a 56,000-seat oval stadium that features a 175m leaning tower. Visible in the distance are the two pyramid-shaped towers of the Olympic Village, where athletes were housed in 1976. Each year, the stadium hosts different events.

The stadium's tower, which is the tallest leaning tower in the world, was renamed the **Tour de Montréal**. A funicular climbs the structure to an interior observation deck that commands a view of the whole

Hochelaga-Maisonneuve

The Olympic Stadium and its famous leaning tower.

city. Various exhibits are shown on the second floor of the observatory.

The former cycling track, known as the Vélodrome, located nearby, has been converted into an artificial habitat for plants and animals called the **Biodôme de Montréal ★ ★ ★**. This unique 10,000m² museum showcases four very different ecosystems: the Tropical Rainforest, the Laurentian Forest, the St. Lawrence Marine Ecosystem and the Polar World. Each area's realistic micro-climate harbours plants, mammals and free-flying birds.

Built facing Avenue Morgan in 1914, the **Marché Maisonneuve ★** is one of Montréal's many lovely public markets. Since 1995, it has occupied a much newer building than the one next door, where it was once established. The Marché Maisonneuve is in keeping with a concept of urban design inherited from the teachings of the École des Beaux-Arts in Paris, known as the *City Beautiful* movement in North America. It is a mixture of parks, classical perspectives and civic and sanitary facilities. Designed by Cajetan Dufort, the market was Dufresne's most ambitious project. The central **Place**

du Marché is adorned with an important work by sculptor Alfred Laliberté entitled *La Fermière* (The Woman Farmer).

Although small, the **Bain Morgan ★** bath house has an imposing appearance due to its Beaux-Arts elements—a monumental staircase, twin columns, a balustrade on the top and sculptures by Maurice Dubert from France. A bronze entitled *Les Petits Baigneurs* (The Little Bathers) is another piece by Alfred Laliberté. Originally, people came to the public baths not only

to relax and enjoy the water, but also to wash, since not all houses in working-class neighbourhoods were equipped with bathrooms.

Marché Maisonneuve's public square is graced with a remarkable sculpture by Alfred Laliberté, *La fermière* (The Woman Farmer).

Detail of an exterior wrought-iron staircase.

Plateau Mont-Royal

If there is one neighbourhood that best defines Montréal, it is definitely the Plateau Mont-Royal. Thrown into the spotlight by writer Michel Tremblay, one of its illustrious sons, the "Plateau" is a neighbourhood of penniless intellectuals, young professionals and old French-speaking working-class families. Its long streets are lined with duplexes and triplexes adorned with amusingly contorted exterior staircases leading up to the long, narrow apartments that are so typical of Montréal. Flower-decked balconies made of wood or wrought iron provide box-seats for the spectacle on the street below.

The Plateau is traversed by a few major streets lined with cafés and theatres, such as Rue Saint-Denis and Avenue du Mont-Royal, but is a tranquil area on the whole. A stroll through this area is a must for visitors who want to grasp the spirit of the city.

The **Sanctuaire du Saint-Sacrement ★** and its church, Église Notre-Dame-du-Très-Saint-Sacrement, were built at the end of the 19th century for the community of priests of the same name. The somewhat austere facade of the church conceals an extremely colourful interior with an Italian-style decor designed by Jean-Baptiste Resther. This sanctuary, dedicated to the "Eternal Exhibition and Adoration of the Eucharist," is open for prayer and contemplation every day of the week.

Avenue du Mont-Royal ★★ is where the neighbourhood's heterogeneous inhabitants can be found on their way in and out of an assort-ment of businesses, ranging from shops selling knick-knacks for a dollar to used records and books.

Parc La Fontaine ★, the Plateau's main green space, was laid out in 1908 on the site of an old military shooting range. Monuments to Sir Louis-Hippolyte La Fontaine, Félix Leclerc and Dollard des Ormeaux have been erected here. The park covers an area of 36ha and is em-bellished with two artificial lakes and shaded pathways. In winter, the frozen lakes become a large skat-ing rink that is illuminated at night. The Théâtre de Verdure outdoor theatre is also located here. Every weekend, the park is crowded with

Colourful Rue Drolet and its 19th-century working-class homes.

people from the neighbourhood who come here to make the most of beautiful sunny days. The park was named after Sir Louis-Hippolyte La Fontaine (1807-1864), a former Canadian Prime Minister and one of the main defenders of the French language in the country's institutions.

An obelisk dedicated to Général de Gaulle, by French artist Olivier Debré, towers over the long **Place Charles-de-Gaulle**, located alongside Rue Sherbrooke. The monument is made of blue granite and stands 17m high. It was given to the City of Montréal by the City of Paris in 1992, on the occasion of Montréal's 350th anniversary. **Hôpital Notre-Dame**, one of the city's major hospitals, stands across the street. From here, you'll also notice the stately building that housed the former

A spectacular view of the downtown core from atop Mount Royal. (pages 157-158)
© Stéphan Poulin

Bibliothèque Centrale de Montréal ★, which closed following the creation of the Grande Bibliothèque.

Between Boulevard De Maisonneuve, to the south, and Boulevard Saint-Joseph, to the north, **Rue Saint-Denis ★** is lined with numerous outdoor cafés and beautiful shops, established inside Second Empire–style residences built during the second half of the 19th century. Many bookstores and restaurants that have become veritable Montréal institutions over the years are located on this stretch of street.

Rue Drolet features good examples of the working-class dwellings that were built in the Plateau area during the 1870s and 1880s before the advent of the typical two- and three-storey houses with exterior staircases. The colourful houses may surprise you, with their light green, salmon pink, dark blue or violet ivy-covered brick exteriors. Continue north to the corner of Rachel and Drolet streets to get to Église Saint-Jean-Baptiste.

MICHEL TREMBLAY AND MORDECAI RICHLER

Both prolific writers, Michel Tremblay and Mordecai Richler remain icons on Montréal's literary scene. The former is from Plateau Mont-Royal and the latter from Mile-End, two neighbouring working-class districts that were once separated by a cultural and linguistic divide. Both produced deliciously authentic portraits of their respective environments that were as tender as they were biting, and these two recipients of the Governor General's Award have seen their works brought to both the big and small screen. Also an accomplished playwright, Tremblay kicked off his famous six-part Plateau Mont-Royal Chronicles with his delightful novel *La grosse femme d'à côté est enceinte* (*The Fat Woman Next Door is Pregnant*). Richler, for his part, offered an often critical look at his native Jewish community with such mordantly humorous novels as *The Apprenticeship of Duddy Kravitz*.

Église Saint-Jean-Baptiste ★★, dedicated to the patron saint of French Canadians, is a gigantic symbol of the solid faith of the Catholic working-class inhabitants of the Plateau Mont-Royal at the turn of the 20th century who, despite their poverty and large families, managed to amass considerable amounts of money for the construction of sumptuous churches. The exterior was built in 1874. The interior was redone after a fire and is now a veritable Baroque Revival masterpiece designed by Casimir Saint-Jean that should not be missed. The pink-marble and gilded wood baldaquin in the chancel (1915) shelters the altar, which is made of white Italian marble and faces the large Casavant organs—among the most powerful in the city—in the

Lazing the day away in Parc La Fontaine. © Stéphan Poulin

Mount Royal's illuminated cross was erected in 1924.

© Dreamstime.com

Mount Royal

Named Mont Royal by Jacques Cartier when he climbed to its summit in 1535, Mount Royal is an important landmark in the cityscape and the point of reference around which all of the city's central neighbourhoods gravitate. Known simply as "the mountain" by Montrealers, this squat mass, measuring 233m at its highest point, is composed of intrusive rock. A "green lung" visible from many of the city's neighbourhoods, it exerts a positive influence on Montrealers who, as a result, never really lose touch with nature. The mountain actually has three summits; the first is occupied by Mount Royal Park, the second by the Mount Royal Protestant Cemetery, and the third by Westmount, an autonomous city with lovely English-style homes.

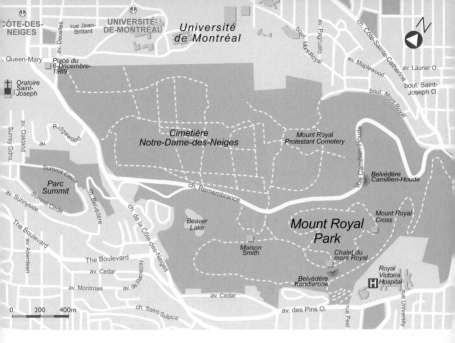

The lovely **Belvédère Camillien-Houde ★★** looks out over the entire eastern portion of Montréal. The Plateau Mont-Royal lies in the foreground, a uniform mass of duplexes and triplexes, dominated in a few places by the oxidized copper bell towers of parish churches, while the Rosemont and Maisonneuve districts lie in the background as the Olympic Stadium towers over them.

The **Mount Royal Cross** was erected on the side of Chemin Olmsted in 1924 to commemorate the moment when the city's founder, Paul Chomedey, Sieur de Maisonneuve, scaled the mountain in January of 1643 to place a wooden cross in thanks to the Virgin Mary for sparing the fort of Ville-Marie from a devastating flood.

Pressured by the residents of the Golden Square Mile, who saw their favourite playground being deforested by various firewood companies, the City of Montréal created **Mount Royal Park ★★★** in 1870. Frederick Law Olmsted (1822-

1903), the celebrated designer of New York's Central Park, was commissioned to design the park. He decided to preserve the site's natural character, limiting himself to a few lookout points linked by winding paths. Inaugurated in 1876, the park, which covers 190ha on the southern part of the mountain, is cherished by Montrealers as a place to enjoy fresh air.

The **Chalet du Mont Royal ★★★**, located in the centre of the park, was designed by Aristide Beaugrand-Champagne in 1932 as a replacement for the original structure, which was about to collapse. During the 1930s and 1940s, big bands gave moonlit concerts on the steps of the building. The interior is decorated with 17 remounted paintings depicting scenes from Canadian history. They were commissioned from some of Québec's great painters, such as Marc-Aurèle Fortin and Paul-Émile Borduas. The exceptional view of downtown from the **Belvédère Kondiaronk ★★★** (named after the Huron-Wendat chief who negotiated the Great Peace treaty in 1701)

Mount Royal

Magnificent Mount Royal Park, the city's "green lung."

is best enjoyed in late afternoon or evening, when the skyscrapers light up the sky.

The **Mount Royal Protestant Cemetery ★★** ranks among the most beautiful spots in the city. Designed as an Eden for the living visiting the deceased, it is laid out like a landscape garden in an isolated valley, giving visitors the impression that they are a thousand miles from the city, though they are in fact right in the centre of it. The wide variety of hardwood and fruit trees attracts species of birds found nowhere else in Québec. Founded by the Anglican, Presbyterian, Unitarian, Methodist and Baptist churches, the cemetery opened in 1852. Some of its monuments are true works of art, executed by celebrated artists. The families and eminent personalities buried here include the Molson brewers, who have the most impressive and imposing mausoleum, shipowner Sir Hugh Allan, and numerous other figures from the footnotes and headlines of history, such as Anna Leonowens, governess of the King of Siam in the 19th century and the inspiration for the play *The King and I.*

The last of the mountain's former farmhouses, today **Maison Smith** is the headquarters of Les Amis de la Montagne, an association that organizes all kinds of exhibits and activities in collaboration with the Centre de la Montagne. Maison Smith also features a permanent exhibit on the flora, fauna, geology and history of Mount Royal.

The small **Beaver Lake** (Lac aux Castors) was created in 1958 in what used to be a swamp. In winter, it becomes a lovely skating rink. This part of the park is laid out in a more conventional manner than the rest, with grassy areas and a sculpture garden.

The **Cimetière Notre-Dame-des-Neiges** ★★, Montréal's largest cemetery, is a veritable city of the dead, as close to one million people have been buried here since it opened in 1855. It replaced the cemetery in Square Dominion (now Square Dorchester), which was deemed too small. Unlike the Protestant cemetery, it has a conspicuously religious character, clearly identifying it with the Catholic faith. Accordingly, two heavenly angels flanking executed by renowned sculptors are scattered alongside the 55km of roads and paths that criss-cross the cemetery.

Parc Summit ★, a veritable urban forest and bird sanctuary, is Westmount's largest park. Its **belvedere** ★★ provides spectacular views of Montréal, especially at sunset.

The magnificent **Oratoire Saint-Joseph** ★★ is topped with a copper dome, the second-largest in the world after St. Peter's in Rome. The oratory stands on a hillside, a location that accentuates its mystical aura, and visitors need to climb some 300 steps to reach its entrance from the gate. It was built between 1924 and 1967 thanks to the efforts of the blessed Frère André, porter of Collège Notre-Dame (across the street), to whom many miracles are attributed. A sprawling religious complex, the oratory is dedicated to both Saint Joseph and its humble creator. It includes the lower and upper basilicas, the crypt of Frère André and a museum. Visitors will also find the porter's first chapel, built in 1904, a cafeteria, a hostelry and a shop selling devotional articles.

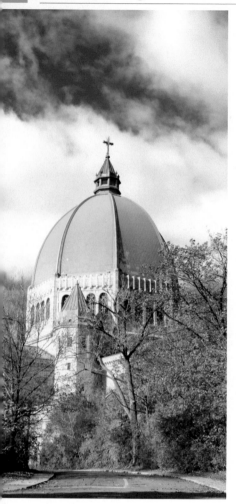

The Oratoire Saint-Joseph's emblematic dome.
© iStockphoto.com / Tony Tremblay

The oratory is one of the most important centres of worship and pilgrimage in North America. Each year, it attracts some two million visitors. The building's neoclassical exterior hides an essentially modern interior. It is well worth visiting the upper basilica to see the stained-glass windows by Marius Plamondon, the altar and crucifix by Henri Charlier, and the astonishing gilded chapel at the back. The oratory has an imposing Beckerath-style organ, which can be heard on Wednesday evenings in summer. Noteworthy aspects of the oratory's exterior in-

a crucifix greet visitors at the main entrance on Chemin de la Côte-des-Neiges.

The "two solitudes" (Canadians of French Catholic extraction and those of Anglo-Saxon Protestant extraction) thus remain separated even in death. The tombstones read like a who's who in the fields of business, arts, politics and science in Québec. An obelisk dedicated to the Patriotes of the rebellion of 1837-38 and numerous monuments

Mount Royal

THE *TAM-TAMS*

The slope of Mont Royal facing Avenue du Parc has been the site of a colourful impromptu party, known simply as the *Tam Tams*, every Sunday afternoon in summer for several years now. Weather permitting, people of all stripes and ages gather here in a bohemian atmosphere.

Dozens of percussionists settle at the foot of the huge monument to Sir George-Étienne Cartier—one of the fathers of Confederation—and improvise lively world-beat rhythms throughout the afternoon. Hordes of dancers groove to the frenzied beat of African congas and other drums, while merry crowds of onlookers enjoy picnics or sunbathing on the grass.

clude its chimes, made by Paccard et Frères and originally intended for the Eiffel Tower, as well as its beautiful Chemin de Croix (Way of the Cross) by Louis Parent and Ercolo Barbieri, in the gardens on the side of the mountain.

The **Université de Montréal** ★ became autonomous in 1920, enabling its directors to develop grandiose plans. Ernest Cormier (1885-1980) was approached about designing a campus on the north side of Mount Royal. The architect, a graduate of the École des Beaux-Arts in Paris, was one of the first to acquaint North Americans with the Art Deco style.

The plans for the main building evolved into a refined, symmetrical Art Deco structure faced with pale-yellow bricks and topped by a central tower, visible from Chemin Remembrance and Cimetière Notre-Dame-des-Neiges. Begun in 1929, construction on the building was interrupted by the stock-market crash, and it wasn't until 1943 that the first students entered the main building on the mountain. Since then, a host of pavilions has been added, making the Université de Montréal the second-largest French-language

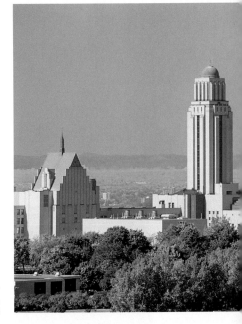

The Université de Montréal's central tower dominates the college campus.
© Université de Montréal

CIMETIÈRE NOTRE-DAME-DES-NEIGES

Cimetière Notre-Dame-des-Neiges (Notre Dame des Neiges Cemetery) was inaugurated in 1855. It is located on land that was created by the thawing of the Laurentide Ice Sheet (a 3km-thick continental glacier) some 10,000 years ago, on the north shore of a lost island in the ancient Champlain Sea (the site of present-day Mont Royal).

On May 29, 1855, Jane Gilroy, the wife of Montréal municipal councillor Thomas McCready, was the first person to be buried in the new cemetery. Her granite monument can still be found on standing on lot F56. Since the burial of Mrs. Gilroy, almost one million people have been laid to rest here, making Cimetière Notre-Dame-des-Neiges one of the largest cemeteries in North America. A walk through the 55km of trails that criss-cross the site provides a reminder that this cemetery is a unique treasure, as much for its architectural, cultural and historical features as for its natural setting.

university in the world, with a student body of over 58,000.

The École Polytechnique of the Université de Montréal, also located on the north side of Mount Royal, was the scene of a tragedy that marked the city and all of Canada. On December 6, 1989, 13 female students and one female university employee were murdered in cold blood inside the École Polytechnique. To keep the memory of these women alive, and that of all female victims of violence, the **Place du 6-Décembre-1989** was inaugurated on December 6, 1999, to commemorate the 10th anniversary of the massacre. There, artist Rose-Marie Goulet erected her *Nef pour Quatorze Reines* (Nave for Fourteen Queens), inscribed with the names of the victims of the Polytechnique massacre.

The splendid Cimetière Notre-Dame-des-Neiges, the final resting place of many illustrious Quebecers.
© Stéphan Poulin

Outremont
and Mile-End

On the other side of Mount Royal is the borough of Outremont, which, like Westmount, clings to the side of the mountain and has, over the course of its development, welcomed a fairly well-off population, including many influential Quebecers.

Outremont was once a municipality and has long been a sought-after residential area. In fact, recent research suggests that the mysterious Aboriginal village of Hochelaga, which disappeared between the voyages of Jacques Cartier and Champlain, was probably situated in this area. Furthermore, Chemin de la Côte-Sainte-Catherine, the main road around which Outremont developed, bears witness to Aboriginal activity in the area and follows a former trail that was cleared by Aboriginals to enable them to skirt the mountain.

Lovely Parc Outremont and its cherub fountain. © Arrondissement d'Outremont

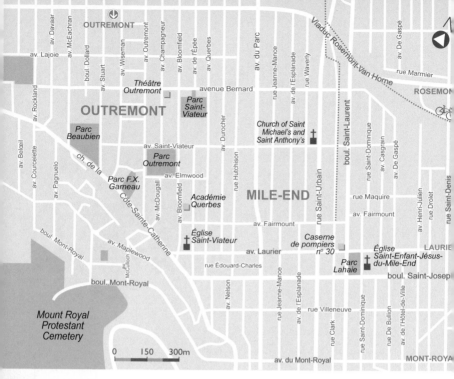

The bucolic landscape of Parc Beaubien.
© Arrondissement d'Outremont

A means of circling the mountain, **Chemin de la Côte-Sainte-Catherine** serves as the border between two types of terrain, while at the same time separating what has come to be known as "Outremont-en-haut" (Upper Outremont), perched atop the mountain, from the rest of the neighbourhood.

Parc Beaubien is located on the site of a farming estate once owned by the prestigious Beaubien family of Outremont, the members of which included several of Québec's prominent social and political figures. The members of the Beaubien clan lived near one another on the hillside; among these were Justine Lacoste-Beaubien, founder of the renowned Hôpital Sainte-Justine for children, and Louis Beaubien, federal and provincial Member of Parliament and his wife, Lauretta Stuart. Louis Riel, the Métis chief from Manitoba whose trial and execution

A well-to-do residence in the peaceful Outremont neighbourhood.

© *Arrondissement d'Outremont*

became famous throughout North America, worked on the Beaubiens' land between 1859 and 1864.

The building that houses Outremont's former **city hall** (1817) alternately served as a warehouse for the Hudson's Bay Company, a school and a prison. A tollbooth used to stand here on Chemin de la Côte-Sainte-Catherine to collect a fee to finance the upkeep of the road, which, like many others in those years, was administered by a private company. The building has returned to its original vocation and now houses the Outremont borough's administrative offices.

The **Pensionnat du Saint-Nom-de-Marie** (boarding school) was built in 1905. Its Renaissance-style portico, silvery roof and dome crowned with a cupola, massive size and elevated location make it stand out on Chemin de la Côte-Sainte-Catherine.

Still higher stands the **Pavillon de la Faculté de Musique** (Faculty of Music), which is part of the Université de Montréal. The pavilion's concert hall, **Salle Claude-Champagne**, is renowned for its exceptional acoustics and is regularly used for recordings. The grounds offer a remarkable view of Outremont, as well as the entire northern part of the island of Montréal.

Outremont and Mile-End

The rich interior of Église Saint-Viateur.

Avenue Claude-Champagne, part of "Outremont-en-haut," is also graced with residential buildings befitting the reputation of this posh neighbourhood. The imposing **Villa Préfontaine** epitomizes the style that many local residents wanted to give their property.

Also known as the "avenue of power," **Avenue Maplewood ★** forms the central axis of the area referred to as "Outremont-en-haut," where various opulent-looking houses with distinctive architecture lie perched in a very hilly landscape, occupied in both the past and the present by influential Quebecers.

Église Saint-Viateur ★★ dates back to the second decade of the last century. Its remarkable interior, inspired by the Gothic Revival style, was decorated by artists renowned in the fields of painting (Guido Nincheri), glass-working (Henri Perdriau), cabinet-making (Philibert Lemay) and sculpting (Médard Bourgault and Olindo Gratton). The ceiling vaults, covered with paintings depicting the life of Saint Viateur, are quite exceptional.

Tango dancers under the arches of Parc Saint-Viateur's white stucco pavilion.

JEWISH COMMUNITIES

Consisting of some 93,000 individuals, the Jewish communities of the island of Montréal are some of the oldest and largest in North America. Of this number, three quarters are Ashkenazi and one quarter is Sephardic. In Montréal per se, Ashkenazi and Sephardic synagogues are mostly located in the Côte-des-Neiges neighbourhood. Since observant Jews can't use cars on the day of the Sabbath, their synagogues must be within walking distance of their homes.

One of the most discreet "visible" minorities in Montréal is the ultra-orthodox Hassidic community, whose 6,000 members mostly live in the Outremont and Mile-End areas, in the heart of the former residential district of Jewish immigrants. Structured around its synagogues and schools, this community does not really blend with the area's other residents, and the urban sector it has occupied since the 1950s stands out with its large number of Jewish establishments.

The overall layout of winding **Avenue Bloomfield** is very pleasant, with large trees, spacious front yards and distinctive architecture. Several buildings are worth a look, including the **Académie Querbes**, built in 1914. The architectural detail—a monumental entrance and stone galleries reaching all the way to the third floor—is quite original for the period. Furthermore, the facilities were ahead of their time, including a swimming pool, bowling alley and gymnasium.

Parc Outremont is one of the neighbourhood's many popular parks, used for both sports and leisure

The charming boutiques and café terraces of Avenue Bernard.   © Philippe Renault

Outremont and Mile-End

activities. Laid out a century ago on swamplands supplied with water by a stream flowing from the nearby hills, it gives the area a serene beauty. Occupying the place of honour in the middle of the Bassin McDougall is a fountain resembling the *Groupes d'Enfants* that adorns the grounds of the Château de Versailles in Paris. A monument to the citizens of Outremont who died during World War I faces the street.

Romantic **Parc Saint-Viateur** features a pond, a small bridge and a pretty white-stucco-covered pavilion built on an islet. The pavilion, which dates from 1927, boasts a surprisingly elegant design for what is essentially a maintenance station. A loggia surrounds its entire structure

and provides a charming spot for a stroll. Tango dancers can sometimes be found here on warm summer nights, while ice skaters make the most of the park in winter.

Avenue Bernard ★ is lined with shops, offices, apartment buildings and houses. This wide avenue with large, grassy medians, curbside landscaping and stately buildings, appears quite imposing and reflects the will of an era to clearly affirm the growing municipality's prestige. The **Théâtre Outremont**, currently a concert hall and movie theatre, is located on this avenue.

Avenue Laurier ★, one of Outremont's trendy shopping streets, is popular with well-off local residents. The avenue has been given a facelift that has contributed to the stylishness of its specialty shops, fashion boutiques, cafes and restaurants.

Visitors can venture east beyond Avenue du Parc to Boulevard Saint-Laurent (with Avenue Fairmount and Avenue Saint-Viateur to the north) to explore the **Mile-End ★** district, a bustling bourgeois-bohemian neighbourhood that has welcomed several waves of immigration in the past. Mile-End is very representative of Montréal's cultural diversity, as much for its residents as for its many businesses, including cafés, restaurants and boutiques that are frequented by a multilingual, eclectic clientele. Most notably, this is where two of the city's culinary institutions can be found: the Fairmount Bagel Bakery and the St. Viateur Bagel Shop. The neighbourhood has a distinctly

working-class flavour, as many factories set up here during the 19th century, most notably quarries and tanneries. The best way to get a feel for the area is to simply stroll down its main streets and savour its eclectic atmosphere.

At the corner of Avenue Laurier and Boulevard Saint-Laurent is a strange castle set up amidst residential buildings. It was built in 1905 and has served several different functions: it has been Saint-Louis-du-Mile-End's city hall, a bank, a post office, a prison and is now a fire station, the **Caserne de Pompiers no 30**. Across Boulevard Saint-Laurent, to the south, is Parc Lahaie, which borders a Baroque-style church: **Église Saint-Enfant-Jésus du Mile-End ★**. The church was built during the 19th century and its dome contains artworks by Ozias Leduc. If

Théâtre Outremont, a National Historic Site of Canada.   © Arrondissement d'Outremont

The Byzantine-style Church of Saint Michael's and Saint Anthony's provides Montréal's skyline with an oriental touch.
© Pascal Biet

there's one church you should visit in the Mile-End, however, it's the **Church of Saint Michael's and Saint Anthony's** ★. The church's construction was overseen by architect Aristide Beaugrand-Champagne, who, surprisingly enough, chose a Byzantine-inspired style for this Catholic church that contrasts sharply with the surrounding working-class residential area. Initially built for the area's Irish community, the church now serves as a place of worship for the neighbourhood's large Portuguese population. Its imposing dome measures 23m in diameter, to which two semi-cupolas were added. Before the Saint-Joseph oratory's construction, this used to be the city's highest domed structure.

Little Italy

Curious visitors and native Montrealers alike flock to the city's *Piccola Italia* for a taste of the Italian way of life.

By the beginning of the 19th century, many of Montréal's best hotels were owned by Italians. At the end of the same century, the first group of immigrants from the poorer regions of southern Italy and Sicily settled in the south-central Saint Jacques neighbourhood, now known as Centre-Sud. The largest wave, however, arrived at the end of World War II, when thousands of Italian peasants and workers set foot on the port of Montréal. Many of them settled around Marché Jean-Talon and Église Madonna Della Difesa, thereby creating Little Italy, where visitors will now find cafés, trattorias and specialty food shops. Since the 1960s, many of Montréal's Italians have moved to the northeastern part of the island, although they still return to Little Italy to do their shopping.

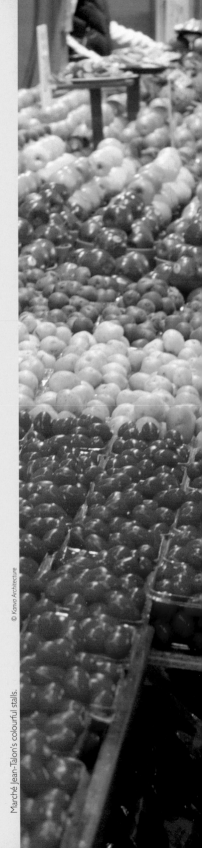

© Kanva Architecture

Marché Jean-Talon's colourful stalls.

Map labels (top to bottom, left to right):

rue Molière
rue De Castelnau E.
rue Drolet
rue Saint-Denis
rue Berri
rue Lajeunesse
av. De Chateaubriand

N

rue Jean-Talon O.
Casa d'Italia
rue Jean-Talon E.
JEAN-TALON

rue Waverly
rue Saint-Urbain
rue Clark
av. Shamrock

Marché
Jean-
Talon

av. Mozart E.
rue Bélanger E.

av. Mozart O.
Parc
Mozart
av. Beaumont

boul. Saint-Laurent

rue Bélanger E.

rue Dante

Église
Madonna
della Difesa

Parc
Dante

Parc
Martel

rue Saint-Zotique E.

rue Saint-Dominique
av. Casgrain
av. De Gaspé
rue Alma
av. Henri Julien
rue Drolet
rue Saint-Denis
rue De Saint-Vallier
rue De Chateaubriand

Plaza Saint-Hubert

rue Beaubien O.

rue Beaubien E.
BEAUBIEN

0   150   300m

Little Italy

Rue Jean-Talon is named after the man who served as intendant (administrator) of New France from 1665 to 1668 and from 1670 to 1672. During his two short mandates, Jean Talon was responsible for reorganizing the colony's finances and diversifying its economy.

The **Casa d'Italia** is the Italian community centre. It was built in 1936 in the Art Moderne style, a variation on Art Deco characterized by rounded, horizontal lines inspired by the streamlined designs of steamships and locomotives. A fascist group briefly took up residence here before the Second World War.

Plaza Saint-Hubert is known for its shops, most of which sell inexpensive, low-quality merchandise. The glass awnings were put up over the sidewalks in 1986.

The design of **Église Madonna Della Difesa ★**, or Our Lady of the Defense church, is of Roman-Byzantine inspiration, characterized by small arched openings and varied treatment of the surfaces, arranged in horizontal bands. A basilica-style plan such as this is unusual in Montréal. The church was designed in 1910 by painter, master glass-worker and decorator Guido Nincheri, who spent over 30 years working on it, finishing every last detail of the decor himself. Nincheri was in the habit of depicting contemporary figures in his stained-glass windows and in his vibrantly coloured frescoes, made with egg-wash, a technique he had mastered. One of these, showing Mussolini on his horse, was a source of controversy for many years. It can still be seen above the high altar.

Parc Dante stretches west of the church, with the place of honour in its centre occupied by a modest bust of the Italian poet, sculpted by Carlo Balboni in 1924. Neighbourhood bocci ball (Italian lawn bowling played on a long narrow dirt court) buffs meet here during the summer months.

Boulevard Saint-Laurent could be described as Montréal's "immigration corridor." Since 1880, immigrants to the city have been settling along different segments of the boulevard, depending on their ethnic background. After several decades, they usually leave the area and scatter throughout the city or reunite in another neighbourhood. Some communities leave few traces of their passage on Boulevard Saint-Laurent, while others have opened shopping areas where descendants of these first arrivals still come with their families. Between Rue De Bellechasse and Rue Jean-Talon, the boulevard is lined with numerous Italian restaurants and cafés, as well

Shopping under the awnings of Plaza Saint-Hubert.
© Plaza Saint-Hubert

as food stores like **Milano**, swarmed by Montrealers of all origins on weekends.

Marché Jean-Talon ★ was built in 1933 on the site of the Irish lacrosse field known as Shamrock Stadium. The space was originally intended for a bus station, which explains the platforms with concrete shelters

Little Italy

The convivial atmosphere at Marché Jean-Talon.
© Stéphan Poulin

over them. The market is a pleasant place to shop thanks to the constant buzz of activity. It is surrounded with specialty food shops, often set up right in the backyards of buildings facing the neighbouring streets. Among these stores, the **Marché des Saveurs**, which stocks a good range of local products, is definitely worth a visit. The market's central area is occupied by farmers who sell their products every day.

Fresh pasta at Milano's Italian grocery store.
© Kanva Architecture

MAJOR THEMES

Montréal's downtown core features a remarkably varied array of architectural styles.

Seasons

FOUR SEASONS AND AS MANY FACES

Montréal is famous for having at least as many moods and sides to its personality as there are seasons in a year. This city truly follows the pace of its often unpredictable climate, and has learned to adapt, and even make the best of it. Temperatures can rise to over 30°C in summer and plummet to less than −25°C in winter, making for markedly distinct seasons; the weather thus influences not only the scenery, but also the lifestyle and behaviour of the local population.

Winter

In winter, the season with which people most commonly associate this "Nordic" city, the temperature often wavers well below freezing and snow falls upon the city, yet Montrealers hardly miss a beat. This is when they head outdoors to enjoy their favourite winter sports, which include cross-country skiing, ice skating and snowshoeing. Montréal is generally hit by four or five snowstorms every winter, and the city has become a world leader in "winter management." When the wind howls and causes blowing and drifting snow, an army of workers is available on call both day and night to remove the approximately 6.5-million cubic metres of snow that, on average, obstruct the city's streets every year.

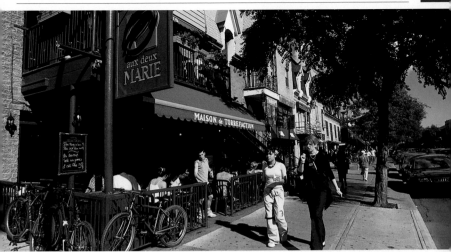

Summer on the Plateau Mont-Royal's Rue Saint-Denis.   © Philippe Renault

Spring

Often abruptly, winter gives way to spring, a brief yet exhilarating season when Montréal takes on the airs of a Mediterranean city. The melting snow gives residents a glimpse of the grass that has turned yellow from the frost and mud, and then nature's awakening becomes spectacular. The first days of the season are always unforgettable, and this is without a doubt the best time to witness how climate can affect people; Montrealers, transformed by the spring sunshine, seem to embrace their Latin roots. They can finally don lighter clothing, lounge on a terrace or stroll through the city. In fact, this is when, after long months of hibernation, a frenzied crowd suddenly takes over Rue Saint-Denis, Boulevard Saint-Laurent and Mount Royal Park. During this lovely prelude to their summer vacations, Montréal residents finally get to enjoy the parks and streets of their city to the fullest.

Summer

In summer, Montréal becomes quite lively, hosting festivals celebrating jazz, comedy and film, as well as Québec's national holiday, all great opportunities to bring hundreds of thousands of people together. Indeed, Montréal summers seem to bring just about everyone out into the streets, and the weather may surprise visitors who see Québec as a land of snow and igloos. The heat can be quite extreme and often seems much hotter because of the accompanying humidity. The vegetation becomes lush, and don't be surprised to see red and green peppers or tomatoes growing in window boxes. City streets are decorated with flowers, and restaurant and terraces are always full, even until the wee hours of the night.

Seasons

The Old Port dons its fall colours.
© Alphonse Tran | Dreamstime.com

Fall

Autumn slowly settles in, and the fall colours can last from September to November. This is when maple trees transform into one of the most beautiful living tableaux on the North American continent. Their leaves take on a kaleidoscope of colours from bright green to scarlet red and golden yellow. The temperatures stay warm for a while, but the days and especially the nights eventually become quite cool. Thus, the seasonal cycle starts anew.

Indian Summer

This relatively short period (only a few days) in late fall feels like summer's triumphant return. Referred to as Indian Summer, it is in fact the result of warm air currents from the Gulf of Mexico. This time of the year is called Indian Summer because it marked the last hunt before winter. Aboriginals took advantage of the warm weather to stock up on provisions before the cold weather arrived.

Seasons

THE NATURE OF THE ISLAND'S GREAT PARKS

Mount Royal Park's Beaver Lake.   © Stéphan Poulin

The island of Montréal, as urban as it is, remains an ideal place for nature adventures since it boasts 17 major parks in its centre and surrounding areas. Montrealers and visitors can take advantage of nice days to escape to one of these vast green spaces that are great for a stroll, a picnic or to enjoy their favourite sports. Each park is home to fauna and flora that are unique to their environment and quite interesting to discover. Most feature a pond or a fountain, or are located near a river or a lake.

Mount Royal Park is clearly the most imposing green lung of the city. Its 190ha take up the southern part of the mountain and are home to approximately 700 species of plants, 150 species of birds, such as the red cardinal and the indigo bunting, and some 20 mammals, including foxes. It also features mature oak and maple stands.

Parc La Fontaine, located in the heart of the Plateau Mont-Royal district, is filled with sugar and silver maples. You can also observe great blue herons here. Parc Maisonneuve, for its part, contains a wide variety of mature hardwood and softwood trees, and is home to the whitetail rabbit. Parc Jarry features unique specimens of mature hardwood trees, as well as a pond where ducks can be found in summer. The Pointe-aux-Prairies nature park, located at the eastern tip of the island, is a paradise for bird-watching; its forests and marshes are home to 184 bird species, such as the green heron and the great horned owl. Parc de l'île-de-la-Visitation, part of the historic site of Sault-aux-Récollets, also features its share of aquatic and river birds that are just delighted to be living near the magnificent Rivière des Prairies.

Seasons

© André Pichette

Summer Activities

Swimming

The majority of the city's CÉGEPs and universities have their own sports facilities with a swimming pool that is open to the public. In addition, the City of Montréal has established outdoor swimming pools in many neighbourhoods, which are very popular on hot summer days.

The three Olympic-size pools (recreational, competitive and diving) at Complexe Aquatique de l'Île Sainte-Hélène were inaugurated in 2005 when Montréal hosted the FINA World Aquatic Championships.

Located on the shore of Lac des Deux Montagnes, the fine-sand beach at Parc-Nature du Cap-Saint-Jacques is ideal for swimming. Parc-Nature du Bois-de-l'Île-Bizard also features a lovely beach where you can enjoy various water sports and activities. On Île Notre-Dame, the water at the Parc Jean-Drapeau beach is naturally filtered, allowing beach-goers to swim in clean, chemical-free water.

Golf

The nine-hole Golf Municipal de Montréal lies just east of Parc Maisonneuve. The Club de Golf de l'Île de Montréal is also located in the eastern part of the city. It has two championship-calibre courses and offers all the services and facilities of a professional golf club.

Bird-Watching

The island of Montréal features several natural sites and other unique spots where you can observe birds.

Countless species of birds can be observed along the shores of Lac des Deux-Montagnes in the Parc-Nature du Bois-de-l'Île-Bizard, particularly American coots and several kinds of ducks, while more than 125 species of birds nest in Parc-Nature de la Pointe-aux-Prairies.

More than a 100 species of winged creatures can be observed at the Parc-Nature du Cap Saint-Jacques, mostly

Black-capped chickadee.
© Andre Nantel | Dreamstime.com

wading birds, raptors and other types of aquatic birds. Wood ducks, eagle owls and red-tailed hawks, among others, also take advantage of these natural surroundings.

The Montréal Botanical Garden is visited throughout the winter by numerous winged creatures. If you're lucky, you might spot a hawfinch, a woodpecker, a coal tit or a red-breasted nuthatch.

In-Line Skating

The Highway Code prohibits in-line skating on the streets of Canadian cities, but it is permitted on the city's bicycle paths. On Île Notre-Dame, the Circuit Gilles-Villeneuve attracts skaters in summer, when they have the car-free race track all to themselves.

Rafting

Looking for a refreshing activity for the dog days of summer? Rafting is a fun activity that will appeal to teamwork-oriented thrill-seekers. A few Montréal companies organize excursions on the tumultuous Lachine Rapids.

Hiking

Montréal is easy to explore on foot. However, those who would

A jet boat rides the Lachine Rapids.
© Éric Gervais, Saute-Moutons

like to roam about magnificent green spaces that have yet to be taken over by asphalt and concrete will find that Montréal also has hundreds of kilometres of trails.

Close to the downtown area, Mount Royal Park is an oasis of greenery that is ideal for walking and hiking. The park features about 20km of trails, including many secondary trails, as well as the wonderful Chemin Olmsted and the loop at the top of the mountain.

Parc-Nature de l'Île-de-la-Visitation has 8km of ecological hiking trails. Hikers can explore hilly areas, small patches of undergrowth, the banks of the Rivière des Prairies and the very pretty island itself.

Mount Royal Park, a haven for hiking enthusiasts.
© iStockphoto.com

Parc Maisonneuve has some 10km of hiking trails, including those that criss-cross the 30 or so outdoor gardens of the Montréal Botanical Garden.

There are a few trails running through Parc La Fontaine, where Montrealers come to relax beneath the tall trees or near the lake.

Parc Jean-Drapeau features some 12km of trails, including footpaths, maintained trails and small paved roads.

Parc Angrignon has a number of little paths, as well as the park's small main road, for a total of nearly 10km.

The 14.5km-long path that runs alongside the Lachine Canal, a favourite with cyclists, can also be enjoyed by pedestrians. It links the Old Port to Parc René-Lévesque in Lachine.

Speleology

The Société Québécoise de Spéléologie organizes tours of Eastern Montréal's Saint-Léonard cave. The guided tour of this 10,000- to 20,000- year-old rock formation includes a slide show and the exploration of the cave.

Summer Activities

Parc La Fontaine's bike path is popular with both cyclists and in-line skaters.
© Richard Duchesne

Tennis

Several urban and recreational parks provide tennis courts for enthusiasts in summer. Some have a cover charge; others are free. With indoor and outdoor courts, Parc Jarry's Stade Uniprix is more than well equipped to satisfy tennis buffs at any time of the year. Built for Tennis Canada, which presents the Rogers Cup competition, it is open to the public

Cycling

Montréal boasts some 600km of bicycle paths. The area around the Lachine Canal was redesigned in an effort to highlight this communication route that was so important during the 19th and early 20th centuries. A lovely bike path was laid out alongside the canal. Very popular with Montrealers, especially on Sundays, the path leads from the Old Port to Parc René-Lévesque, a narrow strip of land jutting out into Lac Saint-Louis that offers splendid views of the lake and surroundings. You can head back to the Old Port by following the river via the Pôle des Rapides trail.

In the northern part of the island, a bicycle path follows Boulevard Gouin and Rivière des Prairies and leads to Parc-Nature de l'Île-de-la-Visitation. Continuing alongside the river, the trail then leads to a very peaceful part of Montréal. It is possible to ride all the way to Parc-Nature de la Pointe-aux-Prairies, and from there follow the path to Old Montréal through the southeast part of the city.

Île Notre-Dame and Île Sainte-Hélène are accessible from Old Montréal. The path runs through an industrial area, then through the Cité du Havre before it reaches the islands (cyclists can cross the river on the Pont de la Concorde). The islands are well maintained and are a great place to relax, stroll and admire Montréal's skyline.

Summer Activities

Winter Activities

Tobogganing

Several Montréal parks feature hills that are specially maintained for winter sliding and tobogganing. They are all suitable for families who wish to spend an afternoon under the winter sun; some are more thrilling and are ideal for daredevils. The best hills can be found at Mount Royal Park (near Beaver Lake and facing Park Avenue) and Parc Jean-Drapeau (during the Fête des Neiges).

Ice Skating

Ice skating has not lost any of its popularity in Montréal. This sport is inexpensive and requires a minimum amount of equipment and technique.

During the winter, a number of public skating rinks are set up in the city. Some of the best ones include Mount Royal Park's Beaver Lake, Parc La Fontaine's pond, the Bassin Bonsecours and the one found in Parc Maisonneuve.

The Atrium, located in the 1000 De la Gauchetière building, features a large year-round skating rink with a surface area of 900m². The rink is overlooked by a superb glass dome that lets the sunshine in.

Young Montrealers enjoying their favourite sport on one of the city's many outdoor ice rinks.
© Philippe Renault

Cross-Country Skiing and Snowshoeing

Montréal is full of spots that are easily accessible by bus or metro where you can enjoy lovely cross-country skiing or snowshoeing excursions in settings that often make you forget all about the city. Standing on your skis at the top of Mount Royal and admiring the downtown office buildings is an unforgettable experience that few cities can rival!

The Parc-Nature de l'Île-de-la-Visitation has 8km of cross-country ski trails, enabling skiers to go all the way around both the park and the island after which it is named.

There are nearly 6km of trails in the Montréal Botanical Garden, offering skiers a chance to familiarize themselves with its many different kinds of trees and winter vegetation. Nearby Parc Maisonneuve has about 10km of trails, enabling skiers to go all the way around the park while admiring the Olympic Stadium's tower.

Skiers can explore Mount Royal Park, the city's green lung or, perhaps more appropriately, "white lung" in winter, on over 25km of trails, all the while enjoying exceptional views of the city.

Parc Angrignon has two cross-country ski trails, each approximately 12km long.

Winter Activities

Arts and Culture

CIRCUS ARTS

Cirque du Soleil and Cirque Éloize have given Québec an international presence and recognition the province had never enjoyed before. The talented Québécois artists who stage these shows have gained a solid reputation as they tour the world and perform for millions of people, and their new creations are often premiered in Montréal, much to the delight of the city's lucky residents.

Cirque du Soleil

The idea for Cirque du Soleil came about in 1984 in Baie-Saint-Paul, in the Charlevoix region, where a group of acrobats on stilts were providing entertainment at a country fair; among them were Gilles Saint-Croix and Guy Laliberté, the circus' founder.

Cirque du Soleil's shows combine elements taken from theatre, dance and traditional circuses (an important exception being that they do not feature animals). Their marvellously enchanting and poetic *tableaux vivants* follow a non-stop narrative, with no intermission and no downtime to break up the rhythm.

Today, some 3,000 employees from 40 different countries work together to create, produce and promote the company's various shows. Several permanent performance halls have been set up around the world, though the company remains headquartered in Montréal.

Cirque Éloize's *Rain* has garnered rave reviews as it has travelled the world.
© *Cirque Éloize 2005 - Joke Schot*

Cirque Éloize

Cirque Éloize was founded in 1993 by a few young residents of Îles de la Madeleine, including Jeannot Painchaud, who had moved to Montréal to study at the École Nationale du Cirque (circus school). The company has since been garnering rave reviews all around the world, and the troupe is renowned for the poetry and originality of its shows, in which acrobatics, dance, music and song come together in a beautiful dream-like whole.

In 2005, the circus company came full circle when it set up its permanent residence in the former Dalhousie train station, in Old Montréal, the same site that housed the École Nationale du Cirque from 1986 to 2003.

TOHU, la Cité des Arts du Cirque

TOHU (from the French expression *tohu-bohu*, which means "the chaos that precedes a rebirth") is a non-profit organization that was jointly founded in Montréal in 1999 by En Piste (an association of Québec circus professionals), the École Nationale de Cirque and Cirque du Soleil. Its main goal is to make Montréal a world capital in the field of circus arts, while participating in the revitalization of the surrounding Saint-Michel neighbourhood.

The idea behind this "circus arts district" is to create a single site that would bring together all of the facilities that go into the creation, training, production and promotion of this field of activity. Today, the circus complex includes the world headquarters of Cirque du Soleil and its artists' accommodations; the École Nationale de Cirque, which also includes the offices of the En Piste association; and the TOHU pavilion. The pavilion is the complex's only public space and a unique example of "green" architecture. It doubles as the entrance to the Complexe Environnemental Saint-Michel and features Canada's first circular performance hall and a large outdoor performance space with a collapsible big tent that can seat 1,700 spectators.

Arts and Culture

James Wilson Morrice, *The Old Holton House, Montréal*, around 1908-1909.
Oil on canvas, 60.5 x 73.2 cm; Purchase, John W. Tempest Fund., Coll. The Montreal Museum of Fine Arts
© *Brian Merrett, MMFA*

VISUAL ARTS

Immersed as they were in the era's religious and nationalistic context, 19th-century Québec artworks mostly stand out for their attachment to an outdated aesthetic. Local painters were nonetheless encouraged by important Montréal art collectors and started following more innovative artistic movements around the turn of the 20th century. Landscape artists who celebrated Québec's natural beauty, such as Lucius R. O'Brien, appeared first. Others from the Barbizon School enjoyed some success through their depiction of the pastoral way of life, and subjectivism was progressively introduced by painters such as Edmund Morris.

The symbolist paintings of Ozias Leduc also demonstrated a tendency towards a subjective interpretation of reality, as did the early-20th-century sculptures of Alfred Laliberté. A few of the era's works also show a certain European influence, as is the case with the paintings of Suzor-Coté and, especially, the Matisse-inspired works of James Wilson Morrice. Morrice died in 1924 and is considered by many as the forerunner of Québec's modern art movement. However, several years passed before Québec's artists really caught up with contemporary world trends. Landscape and urban painter Marc-Aurèle Fortin was one of the rare local artists to make an impression during this period.

Arts and Culture

Alfred Laliberté, *Slave to Machinery*, 1929-1935.
Painted plaster, 27 x 14.5 x 11.5 cm; Purchase, William Gilman Cheney Bequest,
Coll. The Montreal Museum of Fine Arts
© *Christine Guest, MMFA*

Marc-Aurèle de Foy Suzor-Côté, *Shepherdess at Vallangoujard* (Seine-et-Oise), 1898.
Oil on canvas, 235.5 x 100.5 cm; Gift of Graziella Timmins
Raymond Estate, Coll. The Montreal Museum of Fine Arts
© *Brian Merrett, MMFA*

Modern Québec art really started affirming itself during the Second World War, with the innovative work of Alfred Pellan and Paul-Émile Borduas. Two major movements achieved prominence during the 1950s. First and foremost was the non-figurative movement, which can be divided into two strands: abstract expressionism, which includes such artists as Marcelle Ferron, Marcel Barbeau, Pierre Gauvreau and, especially, Jean-Paul Riopelle; and geometric abstraction, as typified by artists such as Jean-Paul Jérôme, Fernand Toupin, Louis Belzile and Redolphe de Repentigny. The second major post-war movement was the figurative style, which was adopted by artists like Jean Dallaire and Jean-Paul Lemieux.

These post-war movements continued into the 1960s, as geometric abstraction became even more popular with the arrival of new artists. Etching and engraving techniques became popular, performance art was introduced and contemporary artists started being called upon to provide works of art for public spaces. The diversification of techniques and styles became widespread at the beginning of the 1970s, leading to the field's current state of extreme eclecticism.

Arts and Culture

Collection Mémoire – *L'Œuvre de Gilles Groulx* (Memory Collection – The Works of Gilles Groulx).
© 1982, *Cinémathèque Québécoise / Bernard Fougères*

FILM

Film pioneer Léo-Ernest Ouimet made history in the field of Montréal cinematography by opening the Ouimetoscope in 1906 in a rented theatre, the Salle Poiré. The following year, he had the building de-molished and built one of the first large theatres in North America, with 1,200 seats, on the same site. At the time, movies produced and filmed in Montréal were mostly centered on themes related to news or travelling. Between 1947 and 1953, private movie producers adapted novels and plays that had been quite popular on the radio, such as *Un homme et son péché* (1948), *Séraphin* (1949), *La petite Aurore l'enfant martyre* (1951) and *Tit-Coq* (1953).

Founded on May 2, 1939, the National Film Board (NFB) was first headquartered in Ottawa and then moved to Montréal in 1956 under the direction of Albert Trueman. For several years, however, the pro-duction of French works was rather slim at the NFB, a fact which was soon perceived as federalist propaganda by Montrealers. In 1964, the NFB was divided into two linguistic sectors (anglophone and franco-phone) following the nomination of its first French-speaking com-missioner, Guy Roberge. This marked the beginning of a new era for filmmaking in the metropolis.

Documentaries, innovative animated films, works of fiction filmed in the "Direct Cinema" style and critiques of the era's clergy-domin-ated Québécois society were the main themes chosen by the first filmmakers who worked for the NFB. Gilles Groulx, Claude Jutra, Norman McLaren, Pierre Perrault, Michel Brault (co-director with Perrault of the innovative *Pour la suite du monde*, 1963) and Jean-Pierre Lefebvre were some of the pioneers of this cinematography.

Shooting *The Brainwashers* at the NFB's Animation and Youth Studio.
© *Alain Corneau / 2002, National Film Board of Canada*

Various feature-length films of the past few decades have captured the imagination of Montréal film-goers, most notably those of Oscar winners Denys Arcand (*Le Déclin de l'empire américain*, 1986; *Jésus de Montréal*, 1989; *Les Invasions barbares*, 2003, the first Canadian film to receive the Oscar for best foreign-language film) and Frédérick Back (the superbly animated *Crac!*, 1981; and *The Man who Planted Trees*, 1988), the former for his social criticism and the latter for his take on environmental issues, as well as those of Pierre Falardeau (*Octobre*, 1994; *15 février 1839*, 2001), which provided a fascinating look at some of the tragic events in Québec history.

The city of Montréal also distinguishes itself in the field of cinema thanks to its numerous movie festivals, much to the pleasure of the many film buffs who call the city home. For several years now, Montréal has also been an exceptional location for directors who travel here from all over the world to take advantage of the undeniable quality of the city's specialized labour force and film services.

LITERATURE AND THEATRE

Toward the end of the 18th century and the beginning of the 19th, the oral tradition still dominated literary life in the New World. Later, the legends from this era (ghosts, will-o'-the-wisps, werewolves, the popular *chasse-galerie* legend) were committed to paper, but there was no true literary movement until the end of the 19th century in Québec. At this point, some of the major themes were survival and praise for a simple, religious, country lifestyle.

Arts and Culture

Tradition continued to be the main theme of Québec literature well into the 1930s, though there were several innovative writers worth noting. Émile Nelligan, an early-20th-century poet, was influenced by Baudelaire, Rimbaud and Verlaine. Producing much of his work early on in life, he slowly sank into madness and today remains a mythical figure. Though country life remained a main feature in the novels of the time, it began to be depicted more realistically, as in *Maria Chapdelaine* (1916) by Louis Hémon, while Albert Laberge's writing (*La Scouine*, 1918) tended to describe its mediocrity.

Québec poet Émile Nelligan.
© *Bibliothèque et Archives Québec*

Literary works began to evolve toward modernism during the economic crisis and the Second World War. The era's literature still featured a predominantly rural setting, though the theme of individual alienation gradually started to appear. Novels set in the city, where the majority of the population now lived, began to appear. This is the case for *Bonheur d'occasion* (*The Tin Flute*) (1945) by Franco-Manitoban Gabrielle Roy, who depicts with great accuracy the despair of a large family living in the Saint-Henri neighbourhood, still today one of the poorest in Montréal.

On the Anglo side, the sharply comic prose of Mordecai Richler (1931-2001), as salty as smoked meat on rye, depicts life in the cold-water flats and small kosher delis of mid-town Montréal in the 1950s. Novels such as *The Apprenticeship of Duddy Kravitz* (1959), *The Street* (1969) and *St. Urbain's Horseman* (1971) portray a neighbourhood whose face has now changed but is still recognizable on certain street corners, such as Clark and Fairmount. Richler was also a frequent contributor to the *New Yorker*, where he gave his controversial accounts of Québec politics. Other well-known literary voices of English Montréal include poet Irving Layton, gravel-throated crooner/poet Leonard Cohen, novelist and essayist Hugh MacLennan and poet and novelist Mavis Gallant. On the stage, playwright David Fennario's *Balconville* (1979), which examines the lives of middle-class Anglophones and Francophones in Montréal, is one of the city's best-known works in English.

Modernism took hold at the end of the Second World War, in spite of the strict political regime of Maurice Duplessis. Novels of the time were split into two categories: urban novels such as *Au pied de la pente douce* (1944) by Roger Lemelin and *Les Vivants, les morts et les autres* (1959) by Pierre Gélinas, and psychological novels like Robert Élie's *La Fin des songes* (1950) and André Giroux's *Le Gouffre a toujours soif* (1953). Prolific author Yves Thériault positioned himself somewhat outside these literary streams with the publication of his novels and stories (including *Agaguk* in 1958 and *Ashini* in 1960), which marked a whole generation of Quebecers between 1944 and 1962. Poetry flourished with the emergence of a number of great poets such as Gaston Miron, Alain Grandbois, Anne Hébert, Rina Lasnier and Claude Gauvreau. Gratien Gélinas' *Tit-Coq* marked the birth of Québec theatre, followed by various works by Marcel Dubé and Jacques Ferron. Among the numerous political essays that took position against the Duplessis regime, the most incisive and influential was undoubtedly the *Refus global* (1948), co-authored by a group of "automatic" painters.

During the Quiet Revolution, in the 1960s, political and social changes affected literary creation, leading to the "demarginalization" of authors. Several essays, such as Pierre de Vallières' *Nègres blancs d'Amérique* (1968), bear witness to this turbulent era of cultural upheaval and political opposition. The novel experienced a golden age, and new authors began to establish themselves, such as Marie-Claire Blais (*Une saison dans la vie d'Emmanuel*, 1965), Hubert Aquin (*Prochain épisode*, 1965) and Réjean Ducharme (*L'avalée des avalés*, 1966). Poetry triumphed while theatre also went through an exciting period, with the emer-

gence of Marcel Dubé and the ascension of such new playwrights as the illustrious Michel Tremblay. In addition, many poets, novelists and playwrights began to write in *joual*, the spoken, popular form of Québec French. In 1969, English theatre was properly represented with the creation of the Centaur Theatre Company, which moved into the Old Montréal building that housed Canada's first stock exchange.

Actors Réal Bossé and Salomé Corbo of the *Ligue Nationale d'Improvisation*, a competitive improvisational theatre league.
© *Marie-Lyne Caisse / Ligue nationale d'improvisation*

Contemporary literature became richer and more diverse with the emergence of various new talents, while theatre became a far more important genre during the 1980s, which saw the staging of many quality productions, several of which integrated outside artistic expressions such as dance,

Les Grands Ballets Canadiens performing *Noces*.

song and video. The rising popularity of theatre in Montréal led to the opening of many new venues. Today, the brightest players on Montréal's contemporary theatre scene continue to surprise spectators and fill the city's performance halls.

DANCE

We should not forget to mention the incredible success of classical and modern dance in Montréal. Several companies and troupes, both large and small, ensure the artistic vitality that makes this city a great destination for dancers and choreographers from here and abroad.

Founded in Montréal in 1957 by Ludmilla Chiriaeff, Les Grands Ballets Canadiens has always maintained an unparalleled level of artistic excellence. This exceptional troupe presents classical ballet that is ceaselessly renewed thanks to a strong spirit of innovation. Les Ballets Jazz de Montréal, founded in 1972 by Geneviève Salbaing, explores unique and modern territories in dance. During the 1980s, an explosion of creativity and exploration was set off by the arrival on the Montréal scene of such companies as La La La Human Steps (Édouard Lock, 1980), O Vertigo (Ginette Laurin, 1984), Montréal Danse (Paul-André Fortier and Daniel Jackson, 1986) and Compagnie Marie Chouinard (1990).

MUSIC AND SONG

Music entered a modern era in Québec after World War II. In 1961, Québec hosted an international festival of *musique actuelle* (experimental music). Also in the 1960s, large orchestras, most notably the Orchestre Symphonique de Montréal (OSM), began to attract bigger crowds. We should also mention the ambitious works of classical pianists Alain Lefèvre and Marc-André Hamelin, both of whom are now internationally renowned.

Kent Nagano and the Montreal Symphony Orchestra.   © *Kasskara photographie*

Popular song, which has always been important to Québec folk culture, gained further popularity after World War I thanks to the rise of radio and the improved quality of musical recordings. The greatest success was known by La Bolduc (Marie Travers), who sang popular songs in idiomatic French. During the 1950s, the prevailing popular music trend involved adapting American songs or reinterpreting songs from France. As a result, certain talented Québec songwriters working at the time, like Raymond Lévesque and Félix Leclerc, were virtually ignored until the 1960s.

With the Quiet Revolution, songwriting in Québec entered a new and vital era. Singers like Claude Léveillé, Jean-Pierre Ferland, Gilles Vigneault and Claude Gauthier won over crowds with nationalist and culturally significant lyrics. In 1968, Robert Charlebois made an important contribution to the Québec music scene by producing the first French-language rock album. The annual Saint-Jean Baptiste day celebrations became important happenings that attracted hundreds of thousands of revellers to large outdoor concerts.

French Québec has produced a seemingly endless list of musical stars over the last 30 years, including Jean Leclerc (formerly Jean Leloup), Richard Desjardins, Daniel Bélanger, Lynda Lemay, Yann Perrault, Ariane Moffatt and the Cowboys Fringants. Certain non-Francophone artists like Leonard Cohen, Kate and Anne McGarrigle, Rufus Wainright and Arcade Fire have also enjoyed international success, as has Céline Dion, who sings in both French and English.

The city of Montréal is proud of its two international-calibre orchestras, which are exceptional classical-music ambassadors on the Canadian scene and around the world. Throughout the decades, both have been awarded prestigious prizes for their live performances and high-quality recordings. Founded in 1981, the Orchestre Métropolitain du Grand Montréal, led by Yannick Nézet-Séguin since the year 2000, features 56 musicians who trained in Québec conservatories and music faculties. The Orchestre Symphonique de Montréal (OSM), for its part, has enjoyed, since its foundation in 1934, the kind of musical exposure that befits the greatest orchestras in the world. During the 2006-2007 season, Kent Nagano became the eighth music director for the OSM, succeeding Charles Dutoit.

Arts and Culture

Architecture

By the end of the French Regime, Montréal resembled a typical French provincial fortified town. Within its fortifications were streets lined with churches whose steeples reached above the walls, convents, colleges, hospitals, a few aristocratic and bourgeois homes surrounded by French gardens, a *place d'armes* (parade ground) and a market square.

The architecture of the towns varied little from that of the countryside. The first priority remained the eternal battle against the cold. Added to this, however, was the prevention of fire, which could easily result in tragedy in the absence of an effective fire-fighting system. Two edicts written by New France Intendants in 1721 and in 1727 pertained to construction inside the town walls. Wooden houses with mansard roofs and their dangerous wooden shingles were forbidden; all buildings had to be made of stone and equipped with fire-break walls; attic floors had to be covered with terracotta tiles. Those who could not afford to obey such strict standards built small communities outside the walls. Few examples remain of these wood houses, whose architecture was sober and functional.

The building of the Gothic-Revival-style Église Notre-Dame in Montréal between 1824 and 1829, both of which are, announced the arrival of historicism in Québec architecture. Originally quite marginal, historicism would come to dominate the skyline of Québec's cities and towns in the second half of the 19th century. It is defined by the use of decorative elements taken from different architectural epochs in history, which were popularized thanks to archaeological discoveries, the invention of photography, and the popularity of historical novels across the world.

A typical Montréal triplex building with exterior staircase.
© iStockphoto.com / Galina Barskaya

Colourful architectural elements.
© iStockphoto.com / Galina Barskaya

The Victorian era might seem contradictory; while it looked back in time in terms of its architectural style, it looked decidedly forward when it came to comfort. As such, the technological innovations that made life much more pleasant are often overlooked: running water, automatic hot water heaters, more washrooms, central heating, telephones and electricity.

The attraction of the city proved insurmountable to rural workers, despite meagre wages. These up-rooted people longed for aspects of their country homes in the city: galleries and balconies, numerous well-lit rooms, a lot of storage space, which might also serve as henhouse or stables if necessary. It all had to be inexpensive to heat and relatively easy to maintain. Thus, the Montréal-style dwelling was born. Its outdoor staircases, which wound their way tightly to the second floor in the limited space between the sidewalk and balcony, avoided the need to heat an interior stairwell. Its balconies were reminiscent of rural porches and led directly into the homes (one or two per floor), each of which had their own exterior entrance.

At the beginning of the 1930s, new buildings inspired by the architectural styles of New France were constructed. The 1960s' Quiet Revolution further awakened the province's population to the important traditions of its French heritage. It was the beginning of an era of painstaking restoration.

However, while a part of this heritage was put on a pedestal, another part, that of the 19th century, was increasingly falling under the wrecking ball. The destruction went on until the 1980s. Efforts continue today to stave off the deterioration caused by the massive wave of demolition whose results have been compared to those of a military bombardment, and which left vacant lots scattered across the city.

Architecture

The favourable contacts that Québec architects and artists maintained with their colleagues in Paris, Brussels and London did not deter them from choosing to work in America at the beginning of the 20th century. And so the first skyscrapers pierced the Montréal sky in 1928, following the definitive repeal of a ruling limiting the height of buildings to 10 storeys. This is when Old Montréal, until then considered the nerve centre of the city, was superseded by the development of a commercial sector dominated by Rue Sainte-Catherine. Celebrated architects from the United States designed many of Montréal's towers, giving the downtown core its present, decidedly North-American skyline. The geometric and aerodynamic French Art-Deco style, of which there are several examples in all regions of Québec, was replaced by Modern American architecture following the Second World War. The end of the 1950s saw a new flowering of

Place Ville Marie, one of modern Montréal's most emblematic buildings
© Jean-Francois Dupuis | Dreamstime.com

The luminous Champ-de-Mars metro station.
© Michael Pemberton | Dreamstime.com

the downtown area's urban spaces. The construction of Boulevard Dorchester (now known as Boulevard René-Lévesque) led to the erection of Place Ville Marie, which opened its doors in 1962. Finally, the 1966 inauguration of the city's metro and the 1967 Universal Exposition presented the perfect opportunity to provide Montréal with bold examples of international architecture.

At the beginning of the 1980s, the weariness resulting from the *ad nauseam* repetition of the same formulas put forward by the modernists provoked a return to the styles of the past by way of post-modernism, which freely combined reflective glass and polished granite in compositions that echo Art Deco and neoclassicism. For their part, the 1990s and 2000s were characterized by two opposing ideas: the culmination of post-modernism in the form of a traditional Romantic architecture, and the search for a new ultra-modern style of architecture that made use of new materials.

In 2006, Montréal was named a UNESCO City of Design by the Global Alliance for Cultural Diversity, making it the first North American city to join the U.N. agency's Creative Cities Network in the field of design. The development of the Quartier International de Montréal is considered one of the city's signature architectural achievements in this field.

The Biological Sciences Pavilion at Université du Québec à Montréal.
© *Photo UQAM*

Index

The blue-tinted glass facades of the twin BNP and Banque Laurentienne towers. (pages 202-203)
© David Combes / Dreamstime.com

On summer nights, Montrealers and visitors alike converge on Place Jacques-Cartier. (page 204)
© Stéphan Poulin

Contact Information

Our Offices

Canada: Ulysses Travel Guides, 4176 St. Denis Street, Montréal, Québec, H2W 2M5, ☎514-843-9447, ▤514-843-9448, info@ulysses.ca, www.ulyssesguides.com

Europe: Les Guides de Voyage Ulysse SARL, 127 rue Amelot, 75011 Paris, France, ☎01 43 38 89 50, voyage@ulysse.ca, www.ulyssesguides.com

Our Distributors

U.S.A.: Hunter Publishing, 130 Campus Drive, Edison, NJ 08818, ☎800-255-0343, ▤732-417-1744 or 0482, comments@hunterpublishing.com, www.hunterpublishing.com

Canada: Ulysses Travel Guides, 4176 St. Denis Street, Montréal, Québec, H2W 2M5, ☎514-843-9882, ext. 2232, ▤514-843-9448, info@ulysses.ca, www.ulyssesguides.com

Great Britain and Ireland: Roundhouse Publishing, Millstone, Limers Lane, Northam, North Devon, EX39 2RG, ☎1 202 66 54 32, ▤1 202 66 62 19, roundhouse.group@ukgateway.net

Other countries: Ulysses Travel Guides, 4176 St. Denis Street, Montréal, Québec, H2W 2M5, ☎514-843-9882, ext. 2232, ▤514-843-9448, info@ulysses.ca, www.ulyssesguides.com